SING THEM AGAIN

QUEEN ELIZABETH'S INJUNCTION
TO THE CLERGY,
1559

" FOR the comforting of such as delight in music, it may be permitted, that in the beginning or in the end of the Common Prayer, either at morning or evening, there may be sung an hymn, or such like song, to the praise of Almighty God, in the best melody and music that may be conveniently devised, having respect that the sentence of the hymn may be understood and perceived."

———————

An interesting injunction of 400 years ago at the beginning of the reign of Elizabeth I.

SING
THEM
AGAIN

A Companion to 'Sunday Half-Hour'

by

M. GUTHRIE CLARK, M.A.

HENRY E. WALTER, LTD.
LONDON AND WORTHING

First published 1955
Reprinted 1968

Published by
Henry E. Walter Ltd
26 Grafton Road, Worthing
and printed offset in Great Britain by
The Camelot Press Ltd., London and Southampton

FOREWORD

BY THE

BISHOP OF WORCESTER

IT was Queen Elizabeth I who, four hundred years ago, spoke of hymns being used in the Churches at the beginning and at the end of Morning Prayer, and ever since in varying ways hymn singing in Church has been an act of praise, prayer and thanksgiving. Today they have a recognized place in our services.

Mr. Guthrie Clark has selected some of the best-known hymns, and gives explanations as to their meaning, their use and their origin. These messages are very helpful and illuminating, full of illustrations that would be very useful in Bible Classes and, I think, in the Pulpit too. To interpret hymns to our congregations is both a duty and a difficulty. This book contains about 45 studies, and the selection of the hymns chosen is very good. Well-known hymns, familiar through frequent use, live again. For example, Bunyan's famous hymn, " He who would valiant be," is placed in its setting in *Pilgrim's Progress*, and its meaning stands out clearly in the conversation between Great-heart and Valiant. Isaac Watts' hymn, " When I survey the wondrous cross," lives again in the interpretation given by the author of this interesting book.

We can all recall great occasions when the singing of a hymn in a difficult situation has been of immense importance. I have no hesitation in recommending this book. The mere reading of it will call to our minds the use we can make of many of the hymns here chosen, and, so re-read, their inspiration will grip us in a new way.

WILLIAM WORCESTER.

PREFACE

THE idea which has possessed me as I have prepared these simple talks on some of our best known hymns is that we learn much about God from our hymns, and I have wanted to help readers to understand what they sing. Some of these messages have been preached or passed on in Bible classes; some have been pondered for one's own special profit. Some of the "backgrounds" have been hunted up for one's children or one's friends.

My debt to our greatest authority on hymns, Dr. John Julian, will be seen on every page, and I gladly acknowledge it here. My desire is that these studies will stimulate others to interest themselves in hymns and their writers, and this simple book has been written in the hope that some young people will thus be started on a quest which has never been found fruitless.

There are 45 studies in this book, and every hymn considered is by a different author. But in each case I have mentioned one or two other hymns, of which there is an index, so that we may learn something about the writer even if the hymn itself is not the subject of the study. The arrangement of the series follows the chronological order of the writers, "The Lord is My Shepherd," by David, coming first. The devotional note is struck throughout, because hymns are nothing unless they quicken our devotion to Christ.

To the friends who have helped to prepare my manuscript for the printers I am more grateful than I can say.

M. GUTHRIE CLARK.

CONTENTS

CONTENTS (CONTINUED)

The Lord's my Shepherd

KING DAVID (B.C. 1085-1015)
Sweet Singer of Israel
FRANCIS ROUS
1579-1659

The Lord's my Shepherd, I'll not want:
   He makes me down to lie
In pastures green; He leadeth me
   The quiet waters by.

My soul He doth restore again;
   And me to walk doth make
Within the paths of righteousness,
   E'en for His own Name's sake.

Yea, though I walk through death's dark vale,
   Yet will I fear none ill:
For Thou art with me; and Thy rod
   And staff me comfort still.

My table Thou hast furnished
   In presence of my foes:
My head Thou dost with oil anoint,
   And my cup overflows.

Goodness and mercy all my life
   Shall surely follow me;
And in God's house for evermore
   My dwelling-place shall be.

OTHER HYMNS BY FRANCIS ROUS:

As Pants the Hart for Cooling Streams.
Through All the Changing Scenes of Life.

TUNES: *Crimond.*
            Brother James' Air.
            Covenanters' Tune.

THE above is the Scotch version, the metrical version, of Psalm 23, which has become very popular in England in recent years. You will remember it was used at the wedding of our present Queen in Westminster Abbey, Her Majesty having specially asked for it. It is said that the Psalm is better known

9

in this version than in the authorised version, or the Prayer Book version, which is connected with the name of Miles Coverdale. The Psalm is often asked for at weddings, for which it is very suitable. Quite often the words are not remembered when the question is raised beforehand, but the tune is recalled and hummed over and this gives the clue. The tune is called "Crimond," and apart from Scotland, where the "Messiah" is also sung, this is the usual tune for it.

"We must sing the New Testament," an elder declared to the Rev. J. P. Struthers before a service he was taking in a strange Church. "Very well, we'll do that," he said, "let us begin with the 23rd Psalm and then go on to the 72nd."

This Psalm must be connected with Psalms 22 and 24; they constitute a wonderful trilogy. The Psalm of the Cross (22), is followed by the Psalm of the Crook (23), and then the Psalm of the Crown (24). We see Christ in three aspects here. "Jesus Christ the same yesterday (22) today (23) and forever (24)"; Christ in the past (22), Christ in the present (23), and Christ in the prospect (24). Here is a profitable line of meditation, and if pursued you will see what Struthers meant. What a comfort the truths of this Psalm have been to Christians all down the centuries. It was this Psalm which John Ruskin learnt at his mother's knees and never forgot.

I will not stay to tell you of David, who is called "The Sweet Psalmist of Israel" (2 Sam. 23: 1), whose life story can be gleaned from the Bible, but I will say something of Francis Rous, who gave us this moving metric version.

Francis Rous, Provost of Eton, died 7th January, 1659, nearly 300 years ago. In his last will and testament, dated 18th March, 1657, he speaks of a youth in Scotland, his grandson, "concerning whom it is perchance expected that I should do some great matters for him." But as it was utterly abhorrent to him to give him an estate as the heir of idleness, he left him only as much money as would give him "an answerable education towards a profession." I wonder what Rous would have said if he had known that there were to be many generations of youths in England as well as Scotland whose most precious earthly possession from the cradle to the grave was to be his version of the Psalms!

Rous was born in Cornwall in 1579 and educated at Oxford. A lawyer by profession, he was M.P. for Truro during the reign of James I and Charles I. He was a member of the Long Parliament and of the Westminster Assembly, and was Speaker of the Little Parliament which consisted of 139 persons, " faithful, fearing God and hating covetousness," better known as " The Barebone's Parliament," so called after one of its members, " Praise-God Barbon." He held several appointments under Cromwell, including that of Provost of Eton College, in the Chapel of which he was buried, having died at Acton on 7th January, 1659.

Rous was a godly man. His great wish was that the English Commonwealth should be like the Jewish nation under Joshua. His will closes with these solemn words: " I lay hold of the free grace of God in His Beloved Son as my only title to eternity, being confident that His free grace which took me up lying in the blood of irregeneration, will wash away the guilt of that Estate, and all the cursed fruits of it, by the precious blood of His Son, and will wash away the filth of it by the Spirit of His Son and so present me faultless before the presence of God's glory with joy."

Here are eight lines of Rous' version of the 1st Psalm:

> He shall be like a tree by streams,
>   Of waters planted near,
> Which in his season doth not fail
>   His pleasant fruit to bear:
> Whose leaf shall never fade nor fail,
>   But flourish still and stand:
> Even so all things shall prosper well
>   That this man takes in hand.

Let me attach a brief illustration to each of the five verses:

VERSE 1. A shepherd boy was found dead in the Welsh mountains after very heavy snow storms, gripping the fourth finger of his left hand. His dear ones linked this up with the visit of an evangelist, who had told the children of a Sunday School class to repeat this verse, and as there were five words, to associate them with fingers and thumb of the left hand, touching each as they repeated the text. When they came to the " my " finger, to grip it firmly before passing on.

VERSE 2. In the catacombs at Rome, there are many representations of the Good Shepherd. Very often there are touching epitaphs, " In Christo, in pace " (In Christ, in peace). Realise the constant presence of the Shepherd of Peace. " He makes me to lie down " (in death) . . . " He leadeth me."

VERSE 3. " He restoreth my soul." The Lord is the great restorer; He makes the bitter sweet; His name is Jehovah-Rophi —The Lord that healeth. He displayed His power when Israel was coming out of Egypt as we see in Exod. 15. Connect other Jehovah titles with the verses of this Psalm (see Judges 6: 24, Jeremiah 23: 6, Ezekiel 48: 35, Exodus 17: 15, Genesis 22: 14).

VERSE 4. This was the verse with which Francis of Assissi kept up his spirits on his long journey across Europe to convert the Sultan of Turkey. He was often heard chanting this verse.

VERSE 5. Years ago at a great social gathering in the West of London, an eminent actor was called upon to recite. He chose the 23rd Psalm, which he rendered in such a way as to transport his hearers to the pastoral scene of the East. Then an aged clergyman was persuaded to follow him, and he, too, repeated the well known verses, but with a difference. He was voicing an experience more than describing a scene, and every hearer knew it, not least the actor, who got up and said: " My friends, we have been most impressed. Our old friend has been speaking to our hearts. You see the difference between himself and myself is this — I know the Psalm; he knows the Shepherd."

Who would true valour see

JOHN BUNYAN
1628-1688

Who would true valour see,
    Let him come hither;
One here will constant be
    Come wind, come weather,
There's no discouragement
Shall make him once relent
His first avowed intent
    To be a pilgrim.

Who so beset him round
    With dismal stories,
Do but themselves confound;
    His strength the more is.
No lion can him fright,
He'll with a giant fight,
But he will have a right
    To be a pilgrim.

> Hobgoblin nor foul fiend
>   Can daunt his spirit;
> He knows he at the end
>   Shall life inherit.
> Then fancies flee away!
> He'll fear not what men say,
> He'll labour night and day
>   To be a pilgrim.

TUNES: *Monks Gate.*
         Bunyan

IN the heart of the town of Bedford, near a central square, there stands a noble statue. It is that of the most famous man of the county, John Bunyan, the tinker-allegorist and preacher. Not the least striking feature about this remarkable statue is that he holds a Bible in his left hand and points to it with his right; and there is a look of peace upon the man's face, for the Book is the Book of peace: none other than the Word of God can bring peace to men like John Bunyan, or anyone else for that matter.

The hymn which is to be our study now is found in " Pilgrim's Progress," and was never meant to be sung. It is a challenge to the reader, but a fine hymn nevertheless. One loves to hear boys sing it, and when sung to the tune, " Monks Gate," an old Sussex tune, can be very stirring.

In the immortal allegory the poem is towards the end, where Valiant for Truth has been explaining to Mr. Greatheart how his parents tried to dissuade him from the pilgrimage by telling him of the dangers and difficulties he would have to face, but how he believed what Mr. Tell-true had asserted: " I still believed what Mr. Tell-true had said; and that carried me beyond them all."

Great-Heart: Then this was your victory, even your faith.

Valiant: It was so; I believed, and therefore came out, got into the way, fought all that set themselves against me, and by believing am come to this place.

Then comes the hymn. They came upon the Enchanted Ground next, and doubtless this hymn helped them to get the victory, as it has many another. It was a rough bit of the road, but it was prepared by a song. " The singers went before . . . When they began to sing, there was victory " (2 Chron. 20: 22). It is always like that. " When you are depressed sing a Psalm," said Luther. "When you cannot pray, praise," said Robert Murray McCheyne.

From boyhood John Bunyan felt a deep sense of need which only increased with his years. Associating with bad company, he soon contracted habits of cursing, lying and blasphemy. He was twice nearly drowned, and other providential escapes made him feel God was near him. He tried hard to turn over a new leaf, but it was impossible. But when on a visit to Bedford he heard some women talking as they sat in the sun about "a new Birth, the work of God within their hearts," it was "as if God did make them speak." This was another link in the chain which led him to Christ, but he had a rough passage and many fears. "Grace Abounding" records it all, and it is perhaps the most searching autobiography ever written.

' "O Lord, I beseech Thee, shew me that Thou hast loved me with an everlasting love." I had no sooner said it but, with sweetness, this referred to me as an echo or sounding again, "I have loved thee with an everlasting love." '

The Bedford tinker followed his father's trade. He was involved in the Civil War and was present at the Seige of Leicester. Shortly afterwards, at 19, he married a godly woman, who brought him as dowry two books, which she read to her husband. He came under the influence of holy John Gifford, and joined his Church in Bedford in 1653. He soon became a regular preacher in Bedford and around. Later his wife died, leaving him with four young children, one of whom was blind. But he married again and was very happy.

Soon after the Restoration he was molested in his preaching and convicted in 1660 and committed to Bedford Gaol. He was there twelve years, during which time he wrote many of his books. It was later, during a second period of imprisonment, that he wrote *Pilgrim's Progress*, the first part in 1679, the second in 1685.

The tribute to this great work from the pen of Dr. Thomas Arnold, the great headmaster of Rugby, is worth quoting:

"I have left off reading our divines, but if I could find a great man among them I would read him thankfully and earnestly. As it is, I hold John Bunyan to have been a man of incomparably greater genius than any of them, and to have given a far truer and more edifying picture of Christianity.

His *Pilgrim's Progress* seems to be a complete reflection of Scripture."

The hymn is a call to follow the Master in spite of all perils and temptations. We are to be constant; having put our hand to the plough, we must never look back. *No discouragement* must put us off. There are bound to be many from different quarters, but a deaf ear must be turned to them. *No foe* must hinder us. There are giants within and without. The world, the flesh, and the devil, beset us, but none must stand in our way as we go forward. *No fancy* must deter us. Often our worst enemies are imaginary, our fancies.

It is good to remember that this brave pilgrim song was written in a prison when all those things were against him, but God was for him, and all was well! "Valiant for the Truth!" is a Biblical phrase, and occurs in Jeremiah 9: 3.

Awake my soul, and with the sun

THOMAS KEN
1637-1711

Awake my soul, and with the sun
Thy daily stage of duty run;
Shake off dull sloth, and joyful rise
To pay thy morning sacrifice.

Thy precious time mis-spent redeem;
Each present day thy last esteem;
Improve thy talent with due care;
For the great day thyself prepare.

Let all thy converse be sincere,
Thy conscience as the noontide clear;
Think how all-seeing God thy ways
And all thy secret thoughts surveys.

By influence of the light Divine
Let thy own light to others shine;
Reflect all Heaven's propitious rays
In ardent love and cheerful praise.

Wake, and lift up thyself, my heart,
And with the angels bear thy part,
Who all night long unwearied sing
High praise to the eternal King.

I wake, I wake, ye heavenly choir,
May your devotion me inspire,
That I, like you, my age may spend,
Like you may on my God attend.

ANOTHER HYMN BY THOMAS KEN:
Glory to Thee my God this Night.

TUNES: *Morning Hymn.*
Commandments.

BISHOP KEN'S best known hymns were written for the boys of
Winchester College, and first appeared in his " Manual of
Prayers for Use of the Scholars," published in 1674. He entered
Winchester as a foundation scholar in 1651, when 14 years of
age, and being a God-fearing youth, wrote the prayers and
hymns which were later collected in the Manual. Can we call
these a boy's hymns? If so, no hymns which have stood the
test of time, were written earlier in life, with the possible excep-
tion of those by Isaac Watts. He is said to have accompanied
his own hymns on the viol or spinet, though the tunes used are
unknown, but it is usually thought that the prayers and hymns
were written when he was Fellow of Winchester in 1666.

Born at Berkhamstead in 1637, he was very early made an
orphan, losing both father and mother, and being brought up
by his sister. She became the second wife of Isaac Walton, the
writer of the " Complete Angler." Thus Thomas Ken came
under two great influences, the society which gathered in Isaac
Walton's house (men like George Herbert), and also the library
of his foster-father, in which he was allowed to browse. There
he read the works of the great Puritan, Richard Sibbes, which
made a deep mark upon him.

Let me give a sketch of his career before saying something
of his character and reviewing the hymn which lies before us.
From Winchester School he went to New College, Oxford; was
successively Rector of two parishes, Little Easton in Essex, and
Brighstone. We find him Chaplain to the Princess Mary at
the Hague in 1679. He was consecrated Bishop of Bath and

Wells in 1685; imprisoned in the Tower in 1688, deprived in 1689. He spent the remainder of his days in retirement at Lord Weymouth's seat of Longleat. He died on 19th March, 1711, and was buried at Frome. " God's will be done," were his last words. He put on his shroud before his death, having carried it in his bag for years.

One of the outstanding points about him was his love for the Church of England, and his steadfastness in upholding its reformed character. It was because of this that he refused to read the Declaration of Indulgence in 1688 which meant imprisonment in the Tower. He was averse to Romanism and determined to maintain the freedom of the Church of England.

This refusal was providential. It opened men's eyes to their danger. Beginning on the West Coast, men banded together to march on the Tower of London to release the prisoners, Ken, Bishop of Winchester and Trelawny, Bishop of Exeter, among them. They put their convictions into song:

> " And shall Trelawny die, and must Trelawny die,
> Then 20,000 Cornishmen shall know the reason why."

It is very interesting to see his teaching on the Holy Communion. It is his exposition of the Catechism — called " The Practice of Divine Love " — in which he writes, " Thou who art in Heaven art present throughout the whole sacramental action to every devout receiver." His last testimony was, " As for my religion, I die in the Holy Catholic, Apostolic Faith, professed by the whole Church before the dissension of East and West, more particularly, I die in the communion of the Church of England as it stands distinguished from all Papal and Puritan error and as it adheres to the doctrine of the Cross."

You will be interested to see his ideal for the Ministry:

> " The Clergy the Church Needs, Written
> by Bishop Ken."

" Give me the Priest these graces shall possess: Of an Ambassador the just address . . . A Father's tenderness, a Shepherd's care . . . A Leader's courage, who the cross can bear . . . A Ruler's arm, a Watchman's wakeful eye . . . A Pilot's skill, the helm in storms to ply . . . A Fisher's patience, and a Labourer's toil . . . A Guide's dexterity to disembroil . . . A Prophet's inspiration from above . . . A Teacher's knowledge and a Saviour's love."

He certainly had " a Leader's courage." We see it coming out in his refusal to read the Declaration of Indulgence. Before this he was dismissed from the chaplaincy at the Hague for remonstrating against a case of immorality at the Court. In 1683 when Charles II visited Winchester, bringing the notorious Nell Gwynne with him, Ken refused the King's request to give up his house to the King's paramour. But Charles II bore him no malice, and when the See of Bath and Wells fell vacant, he said, " Where is the good little man who would not give poor Nell a lodging. For he and no other shall be Bishop. I want a man who can tell me my faults."

Is it any wonder that Macaulay says of Ken: " That his character approached, as far as human infirmity would permit, the ideal perfection of Christian virtue . . . he helped on the cause of God more than any man of his time." By certain persons he was called the " Seraphic Ken." Some said of Ken the preacher, " His face was an argument." He had a telling way of putting things and is usually considered one of the masters of the English language. From this point of view it is interesting to remark that James Montgomery calls his hymns " undoubted masterpieces." He had a wonderful way, too, of putting things in sententious epigrams.

> " But God detests his double heart and will,
> He lives two men and yet but one he dies."

I must give you one or two precious morsels that we find mentioned in Plumptre's great biography of Thomas Ken. Every letter he wrote bore the heading, " All glory be to God." On the fly page of his Greek Testament he wrote a text in Latin: *Et tu quaeris tibi grandia? Noli quaerere.* (" And seekest thou great things for thyself? Seek them not ") (Jeremiah 45: 5). He held very generous views regarding the ministry. This comes out in connection with his chaplaincy at the Hague. He regarded the ministers of the Dutch Reformed Church as true ministers. He accepted the principle that each Church had its own laws in this matter, and as long as they were not unscriptural he accepted them.

Coming to the hymn itself, we remark at once that only half of the original hymn is now sung. It is interesting to remember that Ken gave orders that he should be buried in Frome Church early in the morning as the sun rose, the choir and friends singing, " Awake, My Soul and with the Sun." The theme of the hymn is the call to worship God in the morning. The sentiments are not at all unusual, but the hymn has great inspiration because of its simplicity. The Doxology with which it ends has gone round the world and has been sung by myriads. The rhythm and the rhyme is delightfully natural.

(1) *The challenge of the morning.* Every new morning brings a special call to shake off the dull sloth and brace ourselves for duty. We are to offer the many sacrifices: to redeem our time; to keep our conscience clear; to improve our talents; to prepare for the great day ahead; to remember God's presence and His all-seeing eye. All these things are quite ordinary, but how easily forgotten. No wonder Ken urged the boys at Winchester School to repeat this hymn in the early morning.

(2) *The challenge of the angels.* The heavenly choir will be singing God's praise so let us join them. In their unwearied service they are a type of the Redeemer, and we are to fulfil our ministry as they do theirs. Ken practised what he preached. He was always singing. He loved solitude and often was heard singing a solo for God's ear alone in company with angels and archangels. What an inspiration it is to remember our membership of such a choir.

(3) *The challenge of God.* Here is a sublime call to worship and to praise. All the duties of the new born day are to be done in the Light of God Himself, Father, Son and Holy Ghost. Here is the spring and source of them all. There is no blessing which does not originate in Him; there is none who are exempt from praise, for the summons is for all creatures here below.

You may like to see a prayer as well as a hymn he wrote for his boys: " Lord, sanctify us wholly, that our whole spirit, soul and body may become Thy temple. Oh, do Thou dwell in us, and be Thou our God and we will be Thy servants, through Jesus Christ our Lord."

When I survey the wondrous cross

ISAAC WATTS
1674-1748

When I survey the wondrous cross
    On which the Prince of Glory died,
My richest gain I count but loss,
    And pour contempt on all my pride.

Forbid it, Lord, that I should boast,
   Save in the death of Christ, my God;
All the vain things that charm me most,
   I sacrifice them to His blood.

See, from His head, His hands, His feet,
   Sorrow and love flow mingled down;
Did e'er such love and sorrow meet,
   Or thorns compose so rich a crown?

Were the whole realm of nature mine,
   That were an offering far too small;
Love so amazing, so divine,
   Demands my soul, my life, my all.

OTHER HYMNS BY ISAAC WATTS:

Our God Our Help in Ages Past.
There is a Land of Pure Delight.
Jesus Shall Reign, Where'er the Sun.

TUNE: *Rockingham.*

THOSE who have read Arnold Bennett's "Clayhanger" may remember what happened in the Five Towns when the centenary of the Sunday School Movement was observed there. It was a public holiday! Edwin and Hilda, the chief characters in the story, joined the crowds in the streets out of curiosity. They watched the processions and listened to the singing in the most careless way until they heard the words:

"When I survey the wondrous Cross
   On which the Prince of Glory died;
My richest gain I count but loss
   And pour contempt on all my pride."

Hilda, who had never had any interest in spiritual matters, suddenly found herself overwhelmed. As she turned away to conceal her emotions, Edwin asked if she felt all right. Distressed by his want of tact, she blushed, making an effort to relieve her embarrassment by asking who wrote the hymn. Edwin had to admit that he did not know. "Dr. Watts wrote it," she exclaimed, "and it would be worth anything on earth to be able to sing those words, and mean them."

Many have contended that Watts is the greatest English hymn writer. Whether this is true or not I am not prepared to say, but what I can tell you is that he may be regarded as the earliest

writer of hymns in English. Up to the latter half of the 17th
century there were no English hymns except the metrical version
of the Psalter. From 1690, when his first hymn was written,
he poured out a continuous stream of beautiful hymns, including
" Join all the glorious names," " There is a land of pure delight,"
" Jesus shall reign," " Our God our help in ages past." There
is no doubt that the hymn now before us is one which God has
blessed in an extraordinary way. Dr. Julian writes as follows:
" In popularity this hymn is one of the four which stand at
the head of all hymns in the English language. The remaining
three are: 'Awake my soul,' 'Hark the herald angels sing,'
and ' Rock of Ages.' "

Isaac Watts, who was the eldest son of nine children, was
born in Southampton, where his father kept a boarding school.
The boy's bent for poetry soon manifested itself. One day,
during family prayers, he laughed when he saw a mouse run
up the bell rope. When his father demanded an explanation,
he exclaimed quite spontaneously:

> " There was a mouse for want of stairs
> Ran up the rope to say his prayers."

This adding of insult to injury roused his father, who ordered
the boy from the room and took up a stick which was near
at hand. Chastisement was averted because the boy dropped
on his knees, crying:

> " O Father, Father, pity take
> And I will no more verses make."

At 15 years of age he became very serious, a condition of
mind caused by a genuine conviction of sin and need. A year
later the burden fell off as he trusted Christ. " An heir of glory
has been born," he wrote to a friend.

Five years afterwards, when walking back from chapel with
his father, he expressed disappointment about the hymn book
from which they had been singing. " Then, my boy," replied
his father, " the best thing that you can do, is to write some
better ones." In this way Isaac Watts, whom Lord Selbourne
called " The Father of English Hymnology," began that part of
his life-work which has proved most enduring.

Turning to the hymn itself, it is interesting to note two things
about its composition: The first is that the second line of the

opening verse was originally: "Where the young Prince of
Glory died." Then too, there is a further verse, which is usually
omitted. It runs like this:

> "His dying crimson, like a robe
> Spreads o'er His body on the tree;
> Then am I dead to all the globe,
> And all the world is dead to me."

Each verse of this hymn is full of the deepest pathos and
makes its own appeal. I know no hymn which stirs the imagin-
ation more. It transports us to the place called Calvary; the
words make us see what happened. With the eye of the heart
we look upon Him who was pierced for our advantage; time
and place are quickly forgotten as we sing, and we see Him
and find our hearts drawn out in love and adoration.

The hymn suggests three offerings which we should lay down
at the foot of the Cross:

The first is our pride. This, in the Middle Ages, was considered the first of the seven deadly sins. By this sin fell the
angels. It comes direct from hell, says one writer; it is a
spiritual cancer. It is the thing which makes fellowship with
God impossible. We are to pour contempt upon it—it must go.

Then there is the second offering: The vain things which
charm us most. In the city of Florence in the 15th century, the
sermons of Savonarola made a deep impression and the people
decided to burn their vanities as they did at Ephesus in Paul's
day. Upon the Bonfire of Vanities they threw all their bad
books, wicked pictures, gambling games, etc. They were sacri-
ficed in view of His sacrifice.

Finally, love so amazing as Christ's dying love, demands my
all. In face of the great love wherewith He loved us, there
could be nothing but a grateful and wholehearted response.
Where there had been no holding back on His part, there should
be no reservation on ours.

I began this message with fiction, let me end it with fact.

In the year 1888, the poet Matthew Arnold was in Liverpool
to meet his daughter who was returning from America. He
heard Dr. John Watson — or Ian Maclaren, to use his pen
name — preach on the subject, "The Shadow of the Cross."
One of his illustrations was taken from the reports of the Riviera
earthquake. In one place everything but a huge crucifix, erected
by the roadside, fell to the ground; with the earth trembling

beneath them, the people in the neighbourhood rushed to this refuge for protection and help.

The arrow found its mark, and the window let in light. Later that day, Arnold was heard humming the tune and repeating the story which had impressed his mind . " Ah, yes," he urged, " the Cross still stands, and in the straits of the soul, makes its ancient appeal."

An hour later he was dead as the result of heart failure, trusting, we hope, the young Prince of Glory.

Hark ! The glad sound ! The Saviour comes

PHILIP DODDRIDGE
1702-1751

Hark! the glad sound! the Saviour comes,
　　The Saviour promised long;
Let every heart prepare a throne,
　　And every voice a song.

He comes the prisoners to release
　　In Satan's bondage held;
The gates of brass before Him burst,
　　The iron fetters yield.

He comes from thickest films of vice
　　To clear the mental ray,
And on the eye-balls of the blind
　　To pour celestial day.

He comes the broken heart to bind,
　　The bleeding soul to cure;
And with the treasures of His grace
　　To enrich the humble poor.

Our glad Hosannas, Prince of peace,
　　Thy welcome shall proclaim;
And heaven's eternal arches ring
　　With Thy beloved name.

OTHER HYMNS BY PHILIP DODDRIDGE:

O God of Bethel by Whose Hand.
O Happy Day that Fixed My Choice.
Ye Servants of the Lord.

TUNES:　*Bristol.*
　　　　St. Stephen.

The name of Philip Doddridge is a name to conjure with. For the greater part of his life he was associated with the town of Northampton in the Midlands, and one regrets that there is no statue of him there. The figure of Robert Blatchford towers over the main street, but one has to hunt for any trace of Philip Doddridge. One can find the house where he trained candidates for the ministry, and also the Chapel where he preached, both of which are worth a visit. The former always reminds me when I see it of a story which ought not to be forgotten.

A man named O'Connell was convicted of a certain crime and condemned to die. Philip Doddridge, after careful investigation and great expenditure of time and money, proved conclusively that the man could not have committed the crime, being 120 miles from the spot when it happened. But it was too late; judgment had been given and there was no reprieve. Before the man was taken in a cart to the place of execution he was asked if he had any wish, to which he immediately replied that he would like to stop outside the Doctor's house. In that solemn moment, and in the presence of a big crowd, he said, " Dr. Doddridge, every hair of my head blesses you; every throb of my heart thanks you; every drop of my blood adores you. You did your best to save me."

Born in 1702 and dying in 1751, Philip Doddridge lived in very difficult times. Being the last of twenty children he was " thrown aside as dead." His grandfather was a man of the ministry, ejected from the Church of England when the Act of Uniformity was passed. His father, too, was a godly man, who married the daughter of a Bohemian preacher who had to flee for refuge to England. His mother, who died when he was thirteen, taught him the Scriptures from his early days.

He founded an Academy at Northampton for Students and presided over it for 22 years. In the course of that time over 200 students went forth to all parts of England and the Continent. Much attention was given to sermon preparation. " May I remember that I am not here to acquire a reputation but to dispense the Gospel which my Redeemer brought from heaven and sealed with His blood."

He had a delightful sense of humour which was always breaking through. His sister warned him once about some designing female, and she received the witty reply, " Did you ever know

me to marry foolishly in my life?" As a matter of fact he
was very happily married later. Their letters have been preserved and are singularly interesting. Some of the names he
gives her are very curious, such as " Thou dear wretch and
best of women." He calls himself, " Everywhere and always,
invariably your own Doddridge."

He wrote a great deal of poetry, one of his epics being a
great favourite with Dr. Johnson.

> " Live while you live, the epicure would say,
>   And seize the pleasures of the perfect day.
> Live while you may, the sacred preacher cries,
>   And give to God each moment as it flies.
> Lord in my view let faith united be,
>   I live in pleasure while I live to Thee."

In 1750 his heart failed, and a sea voyage was suggested.
He sailed for Lisbon on 14th July, 1751, preaching a farewell
sermon on the words, " For whether we live, we live unto the
Lord: and whether we die, we die unto the Lord; whether we
live therefore, or die, we are the Lord's " (Romans 14: 8). He
died at Lisbon 26th October, 1751.

Doddridge was a prolific hymn writer, and most collections
contain several of his best known hymns. " O God of Bethel "
was a favourite of Dr. Livingstone. " O happy day that fixed
my choice " was chosen by Queen Victoria to be sung at the
confirmation service of one of the Princes. I have chosen the
Advent hymn, " Hark, the glad sound," because it is typical.

This is a hymn to celebrate the first Coming of Christ, and
it does it right well. The note of gladness is struck at the
outset and continues right through the hymn. " Hark the *glad*
sound . . . our *glad* Hosannas." It is one of our most joyful
hymns and the tune " St. Stephen " to which it is sung suits
it well. On account of its simplicity and its " action " — the
action of the Saviour who has come, it is a favourite with
children. Originally there were more verses than we sing at
present, but it is true to say that the verses omitted only expand
the theme without introducing any fresh line of thought. Like
all Doddridge's hymns, it keeps very close to Scripture. Indeed,
many of his hymns were written to emphasize his sermons and
were sung when the sermon was finished. " O God of Bethel "
is the most obvious instance, illustrating Jacob's vow (Genesis
28: 20-22).

Looking more closely at the hymn we see that it begins with the *Fact* of Christ's coming, then turns to the *Purpose* of His coming, and finally the *Consequence*. In connection with the first idea, I like a verse which we do not often sing:

> " On Him the Spirit, largely poured,
>   Exerts its sacred fire;
> Wisdom and might and zeal and love,
>   His holy breast inspire.

As one sings the centre verses one should recall some of the miracles. What works of mercy do we recall as we think of the prisoners, the blind, the broken-hearted! Of course the background passage to which all is related is Isaiah 61: 1, 2. What prisoners were the lepers (Luke 17: 11-19). Think of the faith of the blind man (Mark 10: 46-52). Was anyone more broken-hearted than the widow of Nain whose son was dead? (Luke 7: 11-18).

All Doddridge's hymns can be apprehended in this way, and our author being dead, yet speaketh. Hymnology is a handmaid to meditation, and in this case especially, an inspiration to consecrated evangelism. He comes " to release," " to clear," " to cure."

Jesus lives, thy terrors now

CHRISTIAN FURCHTEGOTT GELLERT
1715-1769

> Jesus lives: thy terrors now
>   Can, O Death, no more appal us;
> Jesus lives: by this we know
>   Thou, O Grave, canst not enthral us.
>   Alleluia!

> Jesus lives: henceforth is death
>   But the gate of life immortal;
> This shall calm our trembling breath
>   When we pass its gloomy portal.
>   Alleluia!

> Jesus lives: for us He died:
>   Then, alone to Jesus living,
> Pure in heart may we abide,
>   Glory to our Saviour giving.
>   Alleluia!

Jesus lives: our hearts know well
    Nought from us His love shall sever;
Life, nor death, nor powers of hell
    Tear us from His keeping ever.
       Alleluia!

Jesus lives: to Him the throne
    Over all the world is given:
May we go where He is gone,
    Rest and reign with Him in heaven.
       Alleluia!

OTHER HYMNS BY C. F. GELLERT:
God is My Song, His Praises I'll Repeat.
To Father, Son and Spirit Praise.

TUNES: *St. Albinus.*
           Lindisfarne.

THE greatest preacher in Birmingham in the last century was Dr. R. W. Dale. One morning when writing his Easter sermon the reality of the Resurrection of Christ broke upon him in a new way. " ' Christ is alive,' I said to myself, ' Alive!' Then I paused, ' Alive!' Can that really be true? Living as really as I am myself? I got up and walked about, repeating ' Christ is living!' At first it hardly seemed true. But at last it came upon me as a burst of sudden glory. Then I said, ' My people shall know it! I shall preach about it again and again, until they believe it as I do now!' " For months afterwards, in every sermon, the living Christ was his one great theme.

It is lovely to recall this story as we come to Gellert's beautiful Easter hymn. It first appeared in English in Miss Cox's *Hymns from the German*, 1841. It was written by Gellert in 1757 when he was Professor of Philosophy at Leipzig. Thus it became known in England. It immediately sprang into prominence and no Easter service is complete without it.

Gellert was born at Hainichen in Saxony, 4th July, 1715, the son of a German pastor. He was marked out for the ministry but nervousness and inability to preach without a manuscript shut his door. But he made his way as Tutor, Lecturer and Professor, first privately and later at his own university. In 1751 he was appointed Extraordinary Professor of Philosophy at Leipzig, and in this capacity he was able to give of his best.

His attachment to his pupils was deep and affectionate. He died in 1769 after a long illness and much suffering.

Remarkable stories are told of his sacrifices and philanthropies. Towards the end of his life when famine swept across Western Germany he gave all he possessed to succour the impoverished around him. And he did it to such a degree that he himself became destitute. When Prince Henry of Prussia passed through the neighbourhood and asked for the poet, he found him in a cold, empty room without any food, but with the manuscript of a hymn before him which he had just completed.

> " I have had my days of blessing,
>   All the joys of life possessing,
>   Unnumbered they appear.
>   Then let faith and patience cheer me,
>   Now that trials gather near me,
>   Where is life without a tear?"

Gellert wrote many books and much sacred poetry. His best known prose work, " The Fables," published in 1846, is still ranked among the classics of German literature. Their simplicity, charm and humour ensure their literary immortality.

Perhaps an extract from the *Dictionary of German Biographies* will give more insight into the man and his work than anything I can say:

" As a hymn writer he also marks an epoch; and while in the revival of churchly feeling the hymns of the Rationalistic period of 1760-1820 have been ignored by many recent compilers, yet the greatest admirers of the old standard hymns have been fain to stretch their area of selection from Luther to Gellert. He prepared himself by prayer for their composition, and selected the moments when his mental horizon was most unclouded. He was distinguished by deep and sincere piety, blameless life, and regularity in attendance on the services of the Church."

Looking at the hymn itself we notice that the first two verses assure us that Christ's Resurrection has robbed death of all its terrors. It is to be feared no more, for Christ has conquered it. " O death, where is thy sting?" " All things are yours," wrote St. Paul, " Life . . . death . . . things to come " (1 Cor. 3: 22). Death is no more an enemy but a friend because Christ transformed it. " If any man keep My saying, he shall never see death " (John 8: 51). One always feels that this being true, it is a pity that the second verse refers to " gloomy portal."

Can the portal be so gloomy when the experience is so glorious? Does not the promise, " shall not see death," refer to the portal as well as death itself?

Verses 3 and 4 contain the challenge that as Jesus lives we are to live to Him. " Henceforth unto Him who died and rose again." We see here the claim of the risen Lord upon us. We cannot live unto ourselves any longer, there must be newness of Life, looking unto Jesus. Verse 4 recalls the glorious words at the close of Romans 8, a lovely reference to which comes in *Memorials of Hedley Vicars* (p. 192).

" I do not think I ever told you of Craney's happy death. Shortly before he breathed his last, he asked Dr. Twining to read Romans 8 to him. As he read, the dying man's breath became shorter and his face brighter; and as the last words fell upon his ear, ' Nor height, nor depth, nor any other creature, shall be able to separate us from the love of God, which is in Christ Jesus our Lord,' he said, ' Thank you, sir, that will do,' and died."

The final verse looks on into the boundless future and to the throne where He reigns. Prayerfully the hymn closes with the request that we may go where He is gone and be with Him for ever.

Jesu, Lover of my soul

CHARLES WESLEY
1707-1781

Jesu, lover of my soul,
    Let me to Thy bosom fly,
While the nearer waters roll,
    While the tempest still is high:
Hide me, O my Saviour, hide,
    Till the storm of life be past;
Safe into the haven guide,
    O receive my soul at last.

Other refuge have I none,
    Hangs my helpless soul on Thee;
Leave, ah! leave me not alone,
    Still support and comfort me:
All my trust on Thee is stay'd;
    All my help from Thee I bring;
Cover my defenceless head
    With the shadow of Thy wing.

Thou, O Christ, art all I want;
    More than all in Thee I find:
Raise the fallen, cheer the faint,
    Heal the sick, and lead the blind;
Just and holy is Thy name;
    I am all unrighteousness:
False and full of sin I am;
    Thou art full of truth and grace.

Plenteous grace with Thee is found,
    Grace to cover all my sin;
Let the healing streams abound,
    Make and keep me pure within:
Thou of life the fountain art,
    Freely let me take of Thee:
Spring Thou up within my heart,
    Rise to all eternity.

OTHER HYMNS BY CHARLES WESLEY:
    Hark! the Herald Angels Sing.
    Soldiers of Christ Arise.

TUNES: *Aberystwyth.*
          Hollingside.

ONE beautiful Spring day, when sitting by an open window,
    a gentleman had a strange experience which resulted in
extraordinary consequences.   He was enjoying the beauty and
fragrance of the garden below, seeking by meditation to disperse
his anxiety, when he was disturbed by what seemed to him a
tragedy.   A little bird was being ruthlessly pursued by a larger
and more fierce one: a hawk, by dropping again and again on
its prey, was dealing blow upon blow at a little sparrow, which
could only end in death.   Frantically the little thing tried to
elude its tormentor, but in vain.   Then, just at that moment,
when Mr. Charles Wesley (for that was the man's name) thought
the victim's death inevitable, the sparrow fluttered helplessly
towards him and buried itself in the folds of his coat, where
it was safe.

Wesley was greatly burdened himself at the time, and longing
for the peace and security of a refuge.   This little happening
brought its own message of comfort to his soul, and inspiration
for the hymn about which I want to tell you.   It is said that
he reached for a piece of paper and wrote down these immortal

lines which have been a means of grace to so many. Henry Ward Beecher, the American preacher, used to say that he would rather have written that hymn than enjoy the glories of all the kings that have ever reigned. Charles Wesley wrote over 6,500 hymns, but it is their general excellence, rather than their number, which makes Julian (in his *Dictionary of Hymnology*), call him " the great hymn-writer of all ages."

The background of this hymn, as of all Charles Wesley's hymns, was black in the extreme. Things were dark *nationally;* our country was at a low ebb in the early part of the eighteenth century; we were on the brink of civil war. The year 1745 is always associated with the Pretender and his invasion of England. Corruption and mismanagement were the order of the day in politics. Rotten Boroughs flourished throughout the land. The Test and Corporation Acts were still unrepealed.

Things were dark *ecclesiastically.* Sir William Blackstone, an eminent lawyer of the time, visited every Church in the City of London in the reign of George III, and not a single discourse could he hear which contained more Christianity than the writings of Cicero. It was impossible to tell whether preachers were followers of Mohammed, Confucius, or Christ.

Things were dark *socially.* The distilling of gin had much to do with the sin of England at this time. " Drunk 1d., dead drunk 2d., free straw " — was a notice seen everywhere. Robbery, immorality, murder, were all common. The sport of the day was of the most degenerate kind.

But God had His plans which were quickly coming to maturity. Charles Wesley and his brother John were converted early in 1738, within a few days of each other. These two brothers wrought a great deliverance in the England of their day: John led the people to Christ, Charles made them sing. Both men were needed, for song always characterizes revival. The story of Charles Wesley's conversion is worth hearing.

On Whit-Sunday, 1738, Charles Wesley was desperately ill. He was staying with a Mrs. Bray, whose sister was nursing him. Suddenly an impulse came to this lady that she should speak to Mr. Wesley about the salvation of his soul. She wisely told her brother about her reluctance, but he urged her to go forward, praying for God's help. By God's grace, she pointed her guest to the Lord Jesus Christ, and Charles Wesley passed from spiritual death to life eternal. That was May 21st. Four days later his brother John found the same Saviour, and the brothers began to work together for a common Master.

How marvellously God works, He never does things by halves. He called a poet one week, and a preacher the next, and they toiled side by side for nearly 50 years.

Throughout England of 200 years ago, this hymn was sung by men and women whose chains had fallen off, and whom Christ had made free. Turn to the hymn once again. Imagine you were living a couple of centuries ago and this lovely song were falling on your ear for the first time, the Holy Spirit having convicted you of your sin.

Having told you something of the origin of the hymn let us now seek for its message. What has the hymn to say to us? What did it convey to those who first heard it, and what comfort does it bring to us?

We find here (1) *A Message of Need*: There are many words and phrases in the hymn which emphasize the plight of the sinner: "The storm of life," "my defenceless head," "I am all unrighteousness," "all my sin,"—these are just a few samples of what I mean. The person who is without Christ is in a desperate position.

But we also find (2) *A Message of a Saviour*: How Christ is glorified in each verse! He is the true Lover of the soul; He is the only refuge; He is the healing fountain of life. The fulness of Christ is beautifully expressed in unforgettable words: "Thou, O Christ, art all I want, More than all in Thee I find!"

Then finally, we discover (3) *A Message of Redemption*: The sinner and the Saviour meet and the result is redemption in spiritual experience. "The bosom of Jesus," "the overshadowing wing," "the healing stream," all tell the same precious story. "My need and Thy great fulness meet, and I have all in Thee."

Children of the heavenly King

JOHN CENNICK
1718-1755

Children of the heavenly King,
    As ye journey, sweetly sing;
Sing your Saviour's worthy praise,
    Glorious in His works and ways.

We are travelling home to God,
    In the way the fathers trod:
They are happy now; and we
    Soon their happiness shall see.

Sing, ye little flock and blest;
    You on Jesus' throne shall rest:
There your seat is now prepared,
    There your kingdom and reward.

Lift your eyes, ye sons of light;
    Zion's city is in sight;
There our endless home shall be,
    There our Lord we soon shall see.

Fear not, brethren; joyful stand
    On the borders of your land;
Jesus Christ, your Father's Son,
    Bids you undismay'd go on.

Lord, obediently we go,
    Gladly leaving all below:
Only Thou our Leader be,
    And we still will follow Thee.

OTHER HYMNS BY JOHN CENNICK:
    Lo, He Comes.
Ere I Sleep, for Every Favour.

TUNES: *Innocents.*
        Bewdley.

NOTHING is quite so Catholic or universal as a hymn book.
    Hymns by men of different denominations are found side
by side with those whose theological outlook is, on paper, poles
apart. But they meet within the covers of every hymn book.
One often wonders whether a new approach to Christian unity
might not be found along the line of hymn singing. Maybe
if we got together to sing our great Redeemer's praise we should
realize our unity with Him, and so with one another. In our
hymns the non-essentials which so often divide us are omitted,
and so we are drawn together on the bigger points. It is
possible that the popularity of the Sunday Half-Hour on the
B.B.C. is connected with this fact. Apparently more listen to
this than any other programme, and they must belong to many
different denominations.

B

Open your hymn book anywhere, and you will find evidence of its catholicity. Let me enumerate some hymns and put the denomination of the writer in brackets.

Lead Kindly Light (Anglican).
Jesu, Lover of My Soul (Methodist).
My Faith Looks Up to Thee (Congregational).
For Ever with the Lord (Moravian).
O Love That Will Not Let Me Go (Presbyterian).
Souls of Men Why Will Ye Scatter (Roman Catholic).

This point comes to mind when we consider the hymn of John Cennick, who parted company with John Wesley on matters of doctrine. But it is good to see that Cennick's hymns are retained in Wesley's hymn book! Friends part, but their hymns are inseparable.

John Cennick was born in Reading in 1718, a descendant of a Quaker family, but attached to the Church of England. He spent the early part of his life there working as a land surveyor. When nearly 20, he came under the influence of John Wesley and was converted, having been under conviction of sin for some time. The terrible burden of his sin began to weigh heavily upon him one day as he walked along Cheapside in London, and he felt there was no hope. What an interesting study offers itself in this connection to find out just where outstanding Christian men and women were first awakened. William Wilberforce was convicted by the Holy Spirit as he was travelling across Europe with his friend Milner, and exclaims in his *Journal*, " My sin! My sin!"

Wesley appointed him as a teacher in a school for colliers' children at Kingswood, but he did not stay there long owing to doctrinal differences, and we later find him associated with Whitefield. In 1745 he joined the Moravians and was by them ordained in London in 1749. He died in London 4th July, 1755, aged only 37. In the course of his short ministry he preached in many parts of England, Germany and Northern Ireland.

The hymn before us for which John Cennick is famous appeared first in his collection issued in 1741 entitled " Sacred Hymns for the Children of God." The original version had twelve verses, but we now rarely sing more than six, but all are of equal value and it must have been difficult to select the best six. One writer says he wrote it " Wesleyan length if without Wesleyan felicity." This may be true of some of his lesser known hymns, but certainly not of this one.

Two of our best known graces to be sung came from his pen: " We thank Thee Lord for this our food " and " Be present at our table Lord."

The hymn we are now looking at is quite a regular trymetric hymn, but one of Cennick's characteristics is his peculiar arrangements of rhyme and metre. Take his beautiful evening hymn, which cannot easily be surpassed, as an example. This is a great favourite, more especially among the Free Churches.

Ere I sleep, for every favour
    This day showed
    By my God,
I will bless my Saviour.

O my Lord, what shall I render
    To Thy Name,
    Still the same,
Gracious, good, and tender?

Thou hast ordered all my goings
    In Thy way,
    Heard me pray,
Sanctified my doings.

Leave me not, but ever love me;
    Let Thy peace
    Be my bliss,
Till Thou hence remove me.

Visit me with Thy salvation;
    Let Thy care
    Now be near,
Round my habitation.

Thou my Rock, my Guard, my Tower,
    Safely keep,
    While I sleep,
Me, with all Thy power.

So, whene'er in death I slumber,
    Let me rise
    With the wise,
Counted in their number.

This favourite hymn which I have selected for consideration has the thought of pilgrimage running through it, pilgrimage to the heavenly city. The thought seems to be that of entry into Canaan. We remember how in the book of Joshua we read (22: 10), "They came unto the borders of Jordan." But we are constantly bidden to lift up our eyes from the earthly to the heavenly.

Let us make our way through the hymn, putting it into prose form, a kind of paraphrase.

Upon our journey let us sing Christ's praise continually. The way we are travelling is the one our spiritual forbears trod with whom we shall soon be united in God's Home.

Our goal is in sight, it is just ahead, and there we shall see our Lord as well as our loved ones. Cast away every fear for Christ Himself commands us to go forward. And we will! We will follow Thee as our leader, our file leader, who will bring us safe home. And in faith we are there, and we will sing with them God's most holy praise.

The unity of all who, as children of the heavenly King, are upon this journey, cannot be better expressed than in the words of Adolph Monod, the celebrated French Divine, "All in Christ, by the Holy Spirit; and for the glory of God. All the rest is nothing."

Guide me, O Thou great Jehovah

WILLIAM WILLIAMS
1719-1791

Guide me, O Thou great Jehovah,
  Pilgrim through this barren land;
I am weak, but Thou art mighty;
  Hold me with Thy powerful hand:
    Bread of heaven,
  Feed me now and evermore.

Open Thou the crystal fountain,
  Whence the healing stream doth flow;
Let the fiery, cloudy, pillar
  Lead me all my journey through:
    Strong deliverer,
  Be Thou still my strength and shield.

When I tread the verge of Jordan,
    Bid my anxious fears subside;
Death of deaths and hell's Destruction,
    Land me safe on Canaan's side:
        Songs of praises
    I will ever give to Thee.

OTHER HYMNS BY WILLIAM WILLIAMS:
    Jesus, My Saviour, is Enough.
    Hark! the Voice of My Beloved.

TUNE: *Cwm Rhondda.*

WELSHMEN have always been very keen on singing. It is said
    that the Revival in 1905 was a revival carried along on a
tide of song. The national movement in connection with
Eisteddfods have done much to foster the love of song on the
other side of the Welsh border. Many believe that Wales caught
fire from Luther's hymns and Psalms which his opponents feared
more than his sermons. Of course it must never be forgotten
that many Welsh hymns have never become known in English
for want of a translator.

Julian holds William Williams, the best known of whose
hymns we are considering, in the very highest esteem. He
writes: " Williams of Pantycelyn surpasses all in the expression
of the yearnings of the heavenly homesickness: in devout
tenderness, often rising unto rapture, wherewith his faith clasps
the crucified Saviour, when wrapt in contemplation of the glory
of Jesus as the Head of the Church Militant and Triumphant,
and also in the depth and maturity of his theological thoughts."

To the famous evangelist, Howell Harris, he owed a twofold
debt. Harris was the instrument of his conversion and also
the one who urged at an Association meeting in his presence,
the necessity for better hymns. Soon afterwards Williams wrote a
hymn, " submitted " it, and was encouraged to write others.

A word must be said about Howell Harris, who was one of
the most remarkable men of his day. Let me tell you something that happened in Williams' presence. Harris had become
a captain in the militia when in 1759 fears were on every hand,
coming especially from the direction of France. The preachers,
including Williams, were driven out of Llandovy and were returning to Pantycelyn, Williams' hometown, when they were

met by Harris. He would not hear of retreat, but led the party
back to Llandovy, and began to preach, whereat they were
attacked with stones. " In the name of Heaven's King —
Quiet!" But none gave heed. Whereupon he loosed his cloak
and showed his military uniform and medals, and shouted again
for silence: " In the name of King George." Terrified and
amazed, they dropped back and there was no more disturbance.
This gives us an insight into the character of that courageous
apostolic band of which Williams was one.

He was born near Llandovy in 1717 and ordained in the
Established Church in 1740. He was intended for the medical
profession, but his sudden conversion under Harris' ministry
changed his course. Harris was preaching from a gravestone in
the churchyard when the young medical student passed by, was
arrested, and brought to the Saviour. But although he was
ordained he never got beyond the diaconate on account of his
unwillingness to keep to Church regulations. He was eager to
preach wherever there was an opening, but this displeased the
Bishop. Thus another brilliant man was lost to the Church
of the land, and he became a Calvinistic Methodist.

For 45 years he preached up and down the Principality with
great powers and acceptance. We find him often associated
with George Whitefield, to whom England owes so much. He
also had the encouragement of the Countess of Huntingdon. It
was at her suggestion that he prepared an English hymn book,
" Gloria in Excelsis " (1717), in which some of his hymns appear, including the fine missionary hymn, " O'er the Gloomy
Hills of Darkness." This hymn was written in 1772 and was
a precursor of the Missionary Societies. Previous to this he
had compiled several other hymn books, the best known one
being " Hosannah " in 1759.

Before turning to the hymn at which we are specially looking,
I would like to give you two verses of his great missionary
hymn to which I have just alluded.

> Let the Indian, let the negro,
>   Let the rude barbarian see
> That divine and glorious conquest
>   Once obtained on Calvary:
>   Let the Gospel
>   Loud resound from pole to pole.

Fly abroad, eternal Gospel,
Win and conquer, never cease;
May thy lasting wide dominions
Multiply, and still increase:
May thy sceptre
Sway the enlightened world around.

The theme of this very stirring hymn is the wilderness journey which is regarded as typical of the Christian life, the passing of Jordan being regarded as entrance into heaven.

VERSE 1. We are bidden to contemplate the pilgrim host, hungry, thirsty, weak and in need of a guide. Then we consider the greatness and power and love of Jehovah who has pledged Himself never to fail His people.

VERSE 2. Without water they must die, but the Lord opens the rock and the waters flow and they stoop down and drink and live. Without a guide they must be lost, but the Lord guides by the pillar of cloud by day and at night by fire. " He Himself will be thy strength and stay."

VERSE 3. Jordan at harvest overflows its banks and is impossible to cross. But the Lord makes a way for the faithful who pass into Canaan dryshod to praise Him for evermore.

The famous Welsh tune, " Cwm Rhondda," to which the hymn is now generally sung, has made it better known, perhaps, than ever before.

The composition is simpler in sentiment than any others by Williams, and is certainly one which reveals a grasp of truth and a sweep which have helped to make him known as " The Sweet Singer of Wales."

How sweet the name of Jesus sounds

JOHN NEWTON
1725-1807

How sweet the name of Jesus sounds
In a believer's ear:
It soothes his sorrows, heals his wounds,
And drives away his fear.

It makes the wounded spirit whole,
And calms the troubled breast;
'Tis manna to the hungry soul,
And to the weary rest.

Dear name, the rock on which I build,
  My shield and hiding-place;
My never-failing treasury, fill'd
  With boundless stores of grace.

Jesus, my Shepherd, Husband, Friend,
  My Prophet, Priest, and King,
My Lord, my life, my way, my end,
  Accept the praise I bring.

Weak is the effort of my heart,
  And cold my warmest thought;
But, when I see Thee as Thou art,
  I'll praise Thee as I ought.

Till then I would Thy love proclaim
  With every fleeting breath;
And may the music of Thy name
  Refresh my soul in death.

OTHER HYMNS BY JOHN NEWTON:

Glorious Things of Thee Are Spoken.
Approach My Soul the Mercy Seat.

TUNE: *St. Peter.*

IT is a good thing for all of us that the days of the press-gang are over. They used to be very active in all the ports of the land, and in many coast towns. When a man-of-war was sailing, men were seized and carried off and obliged to serve on board. The author of the hymn of which I want to speak fell into the hands of a press-gang in early life, and was thus forced into the Navy. That is how John Newton began life in an utterly godless way.

His life ended very differently; he died at the age of 82 as Rector of St. Mary Woolnoth, in the City of London. I hope that many of you have seen the epitaph on one of the walls of that Church. I remember being very moved as I looked at it. It runs like this:

JOHN NEWTON,
Clerk,
Once an Infidel and Libertine,
A servant of slaves in Africa,
was
by the mercy of our Lord and Saviour
Jesus Christ
Preserved, Restored and Pardoned
And appointed to preach the Faith he
had so long laboured to destroy.

And this leads me to my first question: *Was there ever so wonderful a change?* He was never tired of dwelling upon it. Reference to his experience occurs frequently in his sermons: " That the most ignorant, miserable and abject of slaves should be plucked from the coast of Africa and appointed the Minister of the Parish of the first magistrate of the first city in the world is a fact I can contemplate with admiration, but never sufficiently estimate."

For the best part of 20 years he was a seaman, and in that calling he sinned to his heart's content, or rather discontent. While at sea, one writer says, he endured the extreme barbarities of a life before the mast; he fell into the pitiless clutches of the press gang; as a deserter from the Navy he was flogged until the blood streamed down his back; and he became involved in the unspeakable atrocities of the African slave trade.

At one stage he actually sold himself into the hands of a negress; he became the slave of a slave. She kept him under her table, where he lived on the crusts that were tossed to him in his degradation.

Look at him later as the honoured Rector of a City Church in London; crowds came to hear him preach, others visit his home to have their spiritual difficulties resolved.

How did this extraordinary change come about?

It happened whilst he was at sea. His ship was gradually filling with water, and it seemed impossible that they should escape. As Newton plied the pumps with others, he said to the Captain, " If this will not do, the Lord have mercy on us." His own words surprised him. " Mercy! What mercy can there be for me?" As their danger decreased, he began to pray and the Lord heard him. Although his case was desperate, in the Gospel he saw a promise of life. On the 10th March, 1748, at the age of 23, he sought and found the mercy he needed, and began life anew with Christ.

We may well ask what prepared the way for such an experience; and that leads to another question:

Was there ever so wonderful an influence? I want to tell you how two godly women helped him — his mother, and his sweetheart. " I was born in a line of godliness and dedicated to God in my infancy," Newton tells us. His mother prayed with him as well as for him. and being an only child, she devoted much of her time to storing his mind with the words of God's book, which are so hard to forget. The seed was then sown which eventually brought the harvest.

Then there was Mary Catlett with whom he fell in love when he was 17, she being four years younger. Bishop Handley Moule speaks of Newton's devotion to Mary as "the one merciful anchor that saved him from final self-abandonment." There is little doubt that the remembrance of Mary kept John Newton back from self-destruction many a time.

But I want now to come to the hymn itself by asking a final question: *Was there ever so wonderful a hymn?*

> "How sweet the Name of Jesus sounds
>   In a believer's ear;
>   It soothes his sorrows, heals his wounds,
>   And drives away his fear."

We are not surprised that Julian in his *Dictionary*, classes this hymn with the "first hymns in the English language." You will never find these lines omitted from any collection of hymns, which is a rare honour. We can make no mistake in adding that this hymn will always be sung while time lasts, perhaps even then, in eternity, we shall hear it!

The Name of Jesus is precious to the believer, "Unto you who believe He is precious." This is how the Christian life begins, when Christ becomes precious. What power that Name has! Are we sad, or wounded, or fearful? Here is the sweet spell "that can be laid on our hearts," which alone can make us well.

In this Name, too, is found the secret of unfailing rest. This is not idleness, but peace in the midst of a busy life, calm at the centre of a whirlwind.

The third verse is full of metaphors: look at them! A foundation, a protection, a supply. Each of these is spoken of. Then we learn of the content of this never-failing treasury: My Shepherd, Husband, Friend. This is what Newton wrote, not Saviour, Shepherd, Friend; no, he writes the word husband, taking a figure from the most intimate and enduring relation of life, and says: "I am that to thee, and that is what I want to be all the time."

In view of all this spiritual plenty, what is our feeling and reaction? Surely, "Weak is the effort of my heart . . . But in the meantime, until we see Him and praise Him as we ought, we will proclaim His love with every fleeting breath." Breath and life are fleeting, not a moment must be lost.

In December, 1807, John Newton fell asleep in Christ, and began to praise Him perfectly in heaven. William Jay of Bath saw him a little before he died; his clear mind had become clouded and his speech uncertain, but the visitor carried away one precious utterance which is unforgettable. Let us cherish Newton's dying words and ourselves remember the two things mentioned. He said to Mr. Jay: " My memory is nearly gone, but I remember two things — that I am a great sinner, and that Christ is a great Saviour."

The God of Abraham Praise

THOMAS OLIVERS
1725-1799

The God of Abraham praise,
Who reigns enthroned above;
Ancient of everlasting days,
And God of love:
Jehovah, Great I AM,
By earth and heaven confess'd: —
I bow and bless the sacred name
For ever bless'd.

The God of Abraham praise,
At whose supreme command
From earth I rise, and seek the joys
At His right hand:
I all on earth forsake,
Its wisdom, fame, and power;
And Him my only portion make,
My shield and tower.

He by Himself hath sworn;
I on His oath depend;
I shall, on eagles' wings upborne,
To heaven ascend;
I shall behold His face,
I shall His power adore;
And sing the wonders of His grace
For evermore.

Though nature's strength decay,
And earth and hell withstand,
To Canaan's bounds I urge my way,
    At His command;
The watery deep I pass,
With Jesus in my view;
And through the howling wilderness
        My way pursue.

The God who reigns on high,
The great archangels sing,
And "Holy, Holy, Holy" cry,
    "Almighty King;
Who was and is the same,
And evermore shall be:
Jehovah, Father, Great I AM,
    We worship Thee."

The whole triumphant host
Give thanks to God on high;
"Hail, Father, Son, and Holy Ghost,"
    They ever cry.
Hail, Abraham's God, and mine,
I join the heavenly lays;
All might and majesty are Thine,
    And endless praise.

OTHER HYMNS BY THOMAS OLIVERS:

Come, Immortal King of Glory.
O Thou God of My Salvation.

TUNES: *Covenant.*
        Leoni.

"I WAS born at a village called Tregonan, in Montgomeryshire,
in 1725. My father died in December, 1729. My mother
was so afflicted on account of his death, that she died of a
broken heart in March following, leaving me and another son,
not two years old, behind her. My mother's father, Mr. Richard
Humphries, took care of my brother, and when he died, left
him to the care of his eldest son."

Thus begins one of the most remarkable pieces of autobiography ever written. It is included in that extraordinary
collection of essays by Thomas Jackson entitled " Lives of the
Early Methodist Preachers," of which Bishop Gore thought so
highly, advising " all candidates for ordination to learn their
art at the feet of Wesley's heroic labourers." Into a life of
74 years, Thomas Olivers crowded labours of an apostolic

character second only to those of John Wesley himself, his beloved leader. At Tiverton one day he bought a horse for £5, which was his companion for 25 years, carrying him, according to his computation, over 100,000 miles!

He tells us that at 18 years of age he was one of " the most profligate and abandoned young men living." He was considered the worst boy in the district for 20 or 30 years. He became an apprentice shoemaker, but his practices were so evil he had to leave the district. Gambling, drunkenness, dancing, immorality, blasphemy, were the order of the day and night; out of sixteen nights and days, " I was fifteen of them without ever being in bed." Deeper and deeper he sank in the mire, but God had not forgotten him.

Living a wild, vagabond life, he drifted into Bristol, or rather one should say, he was divinely led thither. While there he saw a multitude of people in the street and learnt they were going to hear Mr. George Whitefield preach. " Whitefield," I thought, " I have often sung songs about him; I will go and hear what he has to say." The text was, " Is not this a brand plucked out of the fire?" (Zech. 3: 2). " When the sermon began, I was certainly a dreadful enemy to God, and to all that is good; and one of the most profligate and abandoned young men living; but by the time it was ended, I was become a new creature."

The first thing he did following his conversion was to return to the place where he had been living and pay all his debts. " From Shrewsbury I went to Whitchurch, on purpose to pay sixpence." In this way 70 debts were paid. What an object lesson this! A change of heart means a change of conduct. Conversion is the basis of morality.

For nearly 50 years Olivers continued as an itinerant preacher, broken into occasionally by other calls. At one time he was appointed Wesley's corrector of press, but his " errata were insufferable," and he had to retire. I would not like to give the impression that he was no scholar, but he certainly was not at first; later he mastered Hebrew and Greek.

Young people will be interested to hear his views on marriage. He fixed on certain qualities which he felt were essential, and he set them down in order of importance. " The first was grace. I was quite certain, that no preacher of God's Word, on any consideration, should marry one who is not eminently gracious. The

second, that she ought to have tolerably good common sense.
A Methodist preacher, in particular, who travels into all parts,
and sees such a variety of company, I believed, ought not to take
a fool with him. Thirdly, as I knew the natural warmth of my
own temper, I concluded that a wise and gracious God would
not choose a companion for me who would throw oil, but rather
water, upon the fire. Fourthly, I judged that, as I was connected with a poor people, the will of God was, that whoever
I married, should have a small competency, to prevent my
making the Gospel chargeable to any. Having proceeded thus
far, my next inquiry was, ' But who is the person in whom
these properties are thus found in the most eminent degree?'
I immediately turned my eyes to Miss Green, a person of good
family, and noted through all the north of England for her
extraordinary piety. I therefore opened my mind to her; and,
after consulting Mr. Wesley, we were married."

Although Olivers wrote several hymns, he is remembered by
the one we are considering. Lord Selbourne spoke of it as " one
of the noblest hymns in existence." James Montgomery said,
"There is not in our language a lyric of more majestic style,
more elegant thought and more glorious imagery."

The hymn is a translation or an adaptation of the Hebrew
Doxology sung at special festivals. It contains twelve stanzas,
although we seldom use more than six or seven. The tune was
composed by a Jewish Rabbi, Leoni, after whom it is called.
From the start it has been very popular and few hymn books
are without it. It is one of the most stirring hymns we can
sing and in some ways compares with Charles Wesley's " And
can it be." This notable composition has a nobility about it
that carries us forward exultantly until we come to the last
verse, where we join the whole triumphant host in praising
Father, Son and Holy Ghost.

One stanza is not often sung, which I think one of the best.
It runs like this:

> " The God of Abraham praise,
> Whose all sufficient grace,
> Shall guide me all my happy days
> In all my ways.
> He calls a worm His friend,
> He calls Himself my God,
> And He shall save me to the end,
> Through Jesu's Blood."

It is impossible to comment on the separate verses, but I will mention the theme throughout. It is this. The God of revelation is of such a character that His children need have no fear. It is a fear-expelling hymn because it gives us such a vision of God. " Often when I'm tempted," said Martin Luther, " I burst into song." Well, here is a good song to sing. Who can contemplate His face, His power, His grace, and not be strengthened. The verse of Scripture which Thomas Olivers set at the head of his hymn sums it all up: " I am thy shield, and thy exceeding great reward " (Genesis 15: 1).

All hail the Power of Jesus' Name

EDWARD PERRONET
1728-1792

All hail the power of Jesus' name!
 Let angels prostrate fall;
Bring forth the royal diadem,
 And crown Him, Lord of all.

Crown Him, ye martyrs of our God,
 Who from His altar call;
Extol the stem of Jesse's rod,
 And crown Him, Lord of all.

Ye seed of Israel's chosen race,
 Ye ransom'd of the fall,
Hail Him who saves you by His grace
 And crown Him, Lord of all.

Hail Him, ye heirs of David's line,
 Whom David Lord did call;
The God Incarnate, Man Divine,
 And crown Him, Lord of all.

Sinners, whose love can ne'er forget
 The wormwood and the gall;
Go, spread your trophies at His feet,
 And crown Him, Lord of all.

Let every kindred, every tribe,
 On this terrestrial ball,
To Him all majesty ascribe,
 And crown Him, Lord of all.

Oh that with yonder sacred throng,
We at His feet may fall,
There join the everlasting song
And crown Him, Lord of all.

OTHER HYMNS BY EDWARD PERRONET:

The Lord is King.
O Grant Me, Lord, that Sweet Content.

TUNES: *Diadem.*
Miles Lane.
Ladywell.

THERE is no doubt that the Huguenot refugees who came to this country from 1570 onwards greatly enriched the land of their adoption in many ways. All kinds of industries were introduced; for instance, the making of clocks. These were very rare before the French came. The pendulum clock was introduced as far as we know by the Huguenots. Now I say all this because Perronet was descended from the Huguenots. There ran in his veins some of the best blood of France, for that country lost some of its noblest and most learned families after the Massacre of Bartholomew in 1572. His name gives away his French origin.

Vincent Perronet, Edward's father, was born soon after his father came to England in 1680. Vincent was a graduate of Queen's College, Oxford, and was a close friend of Wesley and the Countess of Huntingdon. His son Edward was born in 1726 and educated at home until he too went to Oxford, though this point is a matter of controversy. He subsequently left the Church in which he was born and brought up, and entered the Ministry of Lady Huntingdon's Connexion, after working for some years with the Wesleys. But he did not settle even there, and later we find him a pastor of a small Congregational Church in Canterbury. He died in 1792, and was buried in Canterbury Cathedral; which is a nice indication of the hospitality of the Church of which he said such hard things!

Of course the National Church was in a sorry state in the middle of the eighteenth century, and provided a ready target for any man who wished to do some sharp-shooting.

The " Mitre," a sacred poem, was published in 1757. Of this Julian has a high opinion as a piece of satire. He says,

" It is pungent, salted with wit, gleams with humour, hits off vividly the well-known celebrities in Church and State, and is well-wrought in picked and packed thoughts." In the preface Perronet wrote: " I was born, and am like to die, in the tottering communion of the Church of England, though I disapprove of many of her ways."

He did good work as one of Wesley's preachers, and readers of the *Journal* will recall many references to his name. Here are two:

" From Rochdale went to Bolton, and soon found that the Rochdale lions were lambs in comparison with those of Bolton. Edward Perronet was thrown down and rolled in the mud and mire. Stones were hurled and windows broken."

" Charles and you (Edward Perronet) behave as I want you to do; but you cannot, or will not, preach where I desire. Others can and will preach where I desire, but they do not behave as I want them to do. I have a fine time between the one and the other. I think Charles and you have in the general a right sense of what it is to serve as sons in the gospel; and if all our helpers had had the same, the work of God would have prospered better both in England and Ireland. I have not one preacher with me, and not six in England, whose wills are broken to serve me."

Although Perronet wrote a good many hymns this is the only one which is in use today. Even so the last verse beginning, " O that with yonder sacred throng," was not his own: It is associated with the name of Dr. John Rippon. It is generally sung to the tune " Miles Lane," written by Wm. Shrubsole, at Perronet's request. The tune got its name from the fact that it was used in the Miles Lane Chapel in London.

The hymn has been blessed to many: a lady visitor to the great exhibition at Paris was stricken with a malady which almost took away the power of speech. Weaker and weaker she grew, and the end gradually drew near. One word only escaped her lips, and that word was " Bring — bring — bring —." Flowers, fruit, dainties, treasures from the exhibition were brought, but she still uttered the word, " Bring—." Bewildered and wondering, the watchers noticed the dawning of the Glory. At last the cloud was lifted from the memory, " the string of her tongue was unloosed," and in a clear and deliberate voice she exclaimed, " Bring forth the royal diadem, and crown Him Lord of all," then quietly laid her head upon the pillow and fell asleep. The uttermost longings of her soul were satisfied as she passed " to see the King in His beauty."

Another lovely story comes from the mission field:

The Rev. E. P. Scott was a missionary in North India. Once he went over the frontier to the warlike tribes beyond, taking his violin with him. After two days' travel he met a party of ferocious mountaineers. They rushed at him, pointing their spears at his heart. Expecting nothing but instant death, he shut his eyes, grasped his violin, and began to play and sing, " All hail the power of Jesus' Name." He reached the verse, " Let every kindred, every tribe," and, as nothing had happened, he opened his eyes. To his surprise he saw all the savages seated round him with friendly interest, eager to listen to his music and to hear what he had to say. He stayed with them two years.

The hymn, which is very rich in Scriptural allusion, was suggested to Perronet by the Coronation of George III. " Sirs, I present to you the undoubted King of this realm." These words were seen as a parallel to the challenge, " Behold your King." Maybe a few words on the Scripture passages on which the verses are based will provide a rich meditation. Just as an earthly king is crowned, so Jesus must be. " Crown Him with many crowns." St. Peter makes it very clear exactly what this means. " But sanctify Christ as Lord in your hearts " (1 Peter 3: 15). For the most part the allusions are to various passages in the Revelation given to St. John the Divine, that much neglected book of the New Testament. Perhaps the hymn will drive us back to that portion of Scripture which is the only one with a special blessing attached to the reading of it.

(1) When John saw the risen Lord, he fell at His feet as dead (Rev. 1: 17). But the reference to the angels seems to be Heb. 1: 6, which harks back to Deut. 32: 43, " And let all the angels of God worship Him."

(2) Verse 2 brings us into Rev. 6: 9, and the reference is to the fifth seal. " I saw under the altar the souls of them that were slain for the Word of God." The imagery is that of the Old Testament. The blood of sacrificial victims would run down the altar in the Temple and collect at the foot, and the blood is the life. Thus the martyrs poured out their life for the truth. Jesse was David's father, and we find almost

the exact words of the hymn in Isaiah 11.

(3) Rev. 7: 4. We have one hundred and forty-four thousand of Israel sealed. They were sealed for blessing, having, like the multitude which no man can number, washed their robes and made them white in the Blood of the Lamb.

(4) The thought of Israel continues. Psalm 110 comes to mind which Christ used in controversy with the Jews as we see in Matt. 22: 41-46. But we too are kings because of our connection with Great David's greater Son (Rev. 1: 5).

(5) Wormwood is mentioned in Rev. 8: 11 and gall in Matt. 27: 34. We can never forget what Christ endured for us. The thought of the trophies appears in Rev. 21: 24. " The kings of the earth do bring their glory and honour into it." We ascribe all to the Lamb who is the King.

(6) Verse 6 takes us to Rev. 5. "And they sung a new song, saying, Thou art worthy to take the book, and to open the seals thereof; for Thou wast slain, and hast redeemed us to God by Thy blood out of every kindred, and tongue, and people, and nation: And hast made us unto our God kings and priests; and we shall reign on the earth."

(7) " I could wish myself famous," said Pilgrim in Bunyan's *Pilgrim's Progress,* and we join with Perronet in a similar longing and expectation. You and I must be among them in crowning Him Lord of all in that Everlasting Song.

Hark, my soul, it is the Lord

WILLIAM COWPER
1731-1800

Hark! my soul, it is the Lord;
 'Tis thy Saviour; hear His word;
Jesus speaks, and speaks to thee:
 " Say, poor sinner, lov'st thou Me?

I deliver'd thee when bound,
 And when bleeding, heal'd thy wound;
Sought thee wandering, set thee right,
 Turn'd thy darkness into light.

Can a woman's tender care
 Cease towards the child she bare?
Yes, she may forgetful be,
 Yet will I remember thee.

Mine is an unchanging love,
　　Higher than the heights above,
Deeper than the depths beneath,
　　Free and faithful, strong as death.

Thou shalt see My glory soon,
　　When the work of grace is done:
Partner of My throne shalt be;
　　Say, poor sinner, lov'st thou Me?"

Lord, it is my chief complaint
　　That my love is weak and faint:
Yet I love Thee, and adore;
　　O for grace to love Thee more!

OTHER HYMNS BY WILLIAM COWPER:
　　God Moves in a Mysterious Way.
　　O for a Closer Walk with God.

TUNE: *St. Bees.*

ARE you lonely, depressed, melancholy, sensitive, burdened?
If so, I think this short story will help you. We are to consider one of William Cowper's best known hymns — " Hark! My Soul, it is the Lord."

Cowper was a great poet as well as an outstanding hymn writer. In the middle of the eighteenth century things were at a low ebb, and he struck out and broke the silence. One writer avers that he was the most important poet between Pope and Wordsworth. " Cowper," wrote Sir Walter Scott, " was the forerunner of the great restoration in our literature." " The Task " is one of the pre-eminent poems of the English language; we all remember " John Gilpin " from our school days:

" John Gilpin was a citizen of credit and renown,
　　A train-band captain eke was he of famous London town."

The writer of these lines, and the lovely hymn which now claims our attention, had a very sad life, overshadowed at all times by the menace of insanity. Dryden's terrible statement may well be applied to Cowper: " Great wits are sure to madness near allied." I often wonder what his life would have been had he not been a Christian; Christ, without doubt, saved him from destruction.

One instinctively has a feeling of real sympathy for Cowper, because he lost his mother when he was six years old — " Not

a day passes but what I think of my mother!" said he, fifty
years after her death, to a friend who sent him a photograph
of his mother which filled him with deep emotion, and inspired
him to write the well-known lines:

> "Oh that those lips had language! Life has passed
> With me but roughly since I heard thee last . . . "

His father, to get rid of him, and be relieved of the respon-
sibility, send him to a boarding school, where he was very
unhappy. This greatly aggravated the nervous condition of the
child, and one cannot help associating the temporary loss of
his reason with those early sad experiences.

In 1763, at the age of 32, when under the wise and loving
care of Dr. Cotton of St. Albans, he underwent a change which
the Bible calls conversion, or the New Birth. He had often
been stirred before, but had never found peace. " My sin; my
sin! O for some fountain open for sin and uncleanness!"

One morning, picking up a Bible, and reading at random,
he comes across words which had helped many others: "Being
justified freely by His grace through the redemption that is in
Christ Jesus, whom God hath sent forth to be a propitiation,
through faith in His blood." " Immediately I received strength
to believe," he declares, " and the full beams of the Son of
Righteousness shone upon me. I saw the sufficiency of the
atonement of my pardon in His blood!"

The result was that Huntingdon, to which town Cowper soon
removed, became a paradise, because the heart of its new inhabi-
tant was full of the unspeakable happiness of a true believer.

Nearly 40 years later he had a wonderful experience at his
death bed. It was as if he saw the Saviour and realising his
welcome, exclaimed, " I am not shut out of heaven after all."

This " lyric of great tenderness and beauty," first appeared
in Maxfield's New Appendix, 1768, some five years after his
conversion. There is no doubt that the hymn is a reflection
of his own experience. All the central verses emphasize the
wonder of God's unfailing love. Each verse reminds us of
some well-known passage of Scripture which I propose to bring
to our attention.

The first verse brings to our minds our Lord's words to Peter,
by the lake side after His resurrection. There Peter heard the
voice of the Lord asking him a question: " Simon, Son of

Jonas, lovest thou Me?" When Jesus speaks we must hearken.

The second verse always reminds me of the parable of the Good Samaritan in Luke 10. There we see how on that lonely road from Jerusalem to Jericho a poor traveller, who had suffered so much from highway robbers, was cared for by one who might well have continued on his journey without taking any notice.

Verse 3 is based upon a verse in Isaiah which I propose to give in full: " Can a woman forget her suckling child, that she should not have compassion on the son of her womb? Yea, they may forget, yet will not I forget thee " (Isaiah 49: 15).

The next verse tells of the love of our Lord Jesus Christ which is vast in every direction. The Bridegroom's words in the Song of Solomon (8: 6), are very striking: " Love is strong as death."

There are several places in Holy Scripture which occur to us when we read over the fifth verse, but the most suitable one is the promise of Christ given at the end of Revelation 3: " To him that overcometh will I grant to sit with Me in My throne." That will be glory indeed!

Three years before his death, Cowper lost his lifelong friend, Mrs. Unwin. This sorrow brought him into the deepest gloom, and he believed himself forsaken of God; but this mood did not last, and his end was a triumphant one. Bishop Moule shall tell the story: " A nephew of Mrs. Cowper's, a Mr. Johnson, was watching by his uncle's dying bed. About half an hour before his death, his face, which had been wearing a sad and hopeless expression, suddenly lighted up with a look of wonder and inexpressible delight. It was as if he saw his Saviour, and as if he realised the blessed fact " I am not shut out of heaven after all."

Rock of ages, cleft for me

AUGUSTUS MONTAGUE TOPLADY
1740-1778

Rock of ages, cleft for me,
    Let me hide myself in Thee;
Let the water and the blood
    From Thy riven side which flow'd,
Be of sin the double cure,
    Cleanse me from its guilt and power.

Not the labours of my hands
    Can fulfil Thy law's demands;
Could my zeal no respite know,
    Could my tears for ever flow,
All for sin could not atone,
    Thou must save, and Thou alone.

Nothing in my hand I bring;
    Simply to Thy cross I cling;
Naked, come to Thee for dress;
    Helpless, look to Thee for grace;
Foul, I to the fountain fly;
    Wash me, Saviour, or I die.

While I draw this fleeting breath,
    When my eyelids close in death,
When I soar through tracts unknown,
    See Thee on Thy judgment throne,
Rock of ages, cleft for me,
    Let me hide myself in Thee.

OTHER HYMNS BY AUGUSTUS TOPLADY:

A Sovereign Protector I Have.
A Debtor to Mercy Alone.

TUNES: *Petra* (Redhead).
        Wells.

WAS there ever such a storm? Thunder, lightning, wind and rain. How the lightning rent the skies! How the thunder rolled and reverberated around the combes and gorges. The violence of the storm seemed to be concentrated into that valley. Hills rose on either side to a considerable height, and out from their grassy slopes protruded vast masses of jagged rock. In this weird place — Burrington Combe — Augustus Toplady, then Curate of Blagdon, Somerset, was caught that stormy afternoon. Quickly looking for cover as the storm began to break, he saw a high limestone slab with a fissure down the middle, just large enough shelter for him. As he stood in that refuge from the storm, the words of this well-known hymn came to his mind. Picking up a playing card that lay at his feet on the ground, he wrote down these four verses. This heirloom, I understand, is now in one of the museums of America.

When the hymn was first published in the *Gospel Magazine,* it bore the unusual title, " A living and dying prayer for the holiest believer in the world."

This hymn is one of the most familiar in every hymn book, and deservedly popular, though the word " popular " must be used in a limited sense and interpreted by the character of the hymn. Some years ago the *Sunday At Home* called for a poll regarding hymns. Out of 3,500 who responded, no less than 3,125 gave first place to " Rock of Ages."

One reason why this hymn is so greatly valued is that it meets the need of all : the storm-tossed hearts of rich and poor, men and women, young and old, find that these lines put their own thoughts into words. It was a great favourite with Albert the Good, the Prince Consort, who asked for it in his dying illness. Mr. Gladstone, one of our greatest Prime Ministers, loved it so much that he translated it into Latin, Greek and Italian. It is remarkable that the hymn is easily translatable.

In January, 1866, when the ill-fated " London " was lost in the Bay of Biscay, the last words heard by some survivors as they pushed off from the sinking ship were the words of this hymn, sung with streaming eyes and breaking hearts, as husband and wife, parent and child, shipmate with shipmate, awaited side by side the vessel's final plunge.

More recently, a traveller seeing the worshippers weeping as they sang in an Armenian Church in Constantinople, asked the purport of their song, and found it a translation of the hymn we are now studying:

> " Rock of Ages! Cleft for me,
>   'Twas a woman sung them now;
> Pleadingly and prayerfully,
>   Every word her heart did know:
> Rose the song as storm-tossed bird
>   Beats with weary wings the air;
> Every note with sorrow stirred —
>   Every syllable, a prayer."

The experience of Moses in the wilderness when he was hidden in the rock is brought before us in verse 1. But this scene quickly vanishes and we find ourselves on the green hill where He was the Rock smitten. The actual words " Rock of Ages " are found in the margin of Isaiah 26: 4: " Trust ye in the Lord for ever, for in the Lord Jehovah is the Rock of Ages!"

When a spear was thrust into Christ's side and His heart was pierced, there flowed out both water and blood, St. John tells us. He stood by the Cross and saw it — Toplady saw there a double cure — deliverance from the grip as well as the guilt of sin.

The next verse tells us of things that are insufficient to deal with sin. Our toil, our zeal, our tears — all this and more could never atone for sin. Only One can do that — it is Christ who does it by His blood.

A devoted missionary in China, Miss Lucy Bambridge, tells how an old Chinese woman sought to merit her salvation by digging a well with her bare hands, a well which was 25 feet deep and 10 feet wide. Of course she found no peace or salvation till she heard of the work of Christ. Can we imagine with what relief this woman would sing these words?

> " Not the labour of my hands,
>   Can fulfil Thy law's demands."

Then we sing on, and hear of the way of salvation. We are to come stripped, helpless and foul, having nothing as a plea, clinging, with empty hands to His dear Cross. It is hard to come like that, but it is the only way. " Wash me, Saviour, or I die."

Thus we are assured that the Gospel is for life and death and eternity — a perfect provision. Christ who is our hiding place now, will be our hiding place THEN. And He did it for me!

Let me close this short study by telling you how Toplady came to hide in Christ. It was when he was 16. He was on a visit to Ireland where his mother had an estate. Near to where they were staying in County Wexford, a Methodist preacher named James Morris was holding an evangelistic mission and preaching the gospel in a barn. Augustus Toplady, captivated by the idea of such a novelty, and curious to see it for himself, decided to give the preacher a hearing. That night the missioner seemed inspired as he expounded the words, " Ye who sometimes were far off were made nigh by the blood of Christ." " Under that sermon," he himself said, " Under that sermon I was, I trust, brought nigh by the Blood of Christ. Strange that I, who had so long sat under the means of grace in England, should be brought nigh by the Blood of Christ in an obscure part of Ireland, amidst a handful of God's people met together in a barn, and under the ministry of one who could hardly spell his own name. I shall remember that day to all eternity."

> " Rock of Ages! Cleft for *me*,
>   Let *me* hide myself in Thee."

Our blessed Redeemer, ere be breathed

HARRIET AUBER
1773-1862

Our bless'd Redeemer, ere He breathed
    His tender last farewell,
A Guide, a Comforter, bequeath'd
        With us to dwell.

He came in semblance of a dove
    With sheltering wings outspread,
The holy balm of peace and love
        On earth to shed.

He came sweet influence to impart,
    A gracious, willing Guest,
While He can find one humble heart
        Wherein to rest.

And His that gentle voice we hear,
    Soft as the breath of even,
That checks each fault, that calms each fear,
        And speaks of heaven.

And every virtue we possess,
    And every victory won,
And every thought of holiness,
        Are His alone.

Spirit of purity and grace,
    Our weakness, pitying, see;
O make our hearts Thy dwelling-place,
        And meet for Thee.

OTHER HYMNS BY HARRIET AUBER:

    Bright was the Guiding Star.
    Sweet is the Work, O Lord.

TUNE: *St. Cuthbert.*

SOME have written on stone (like God who wrote the Ten
    Commandments); some have written on papyrus (like Moses
whose work we have in the Pentateuch): some have written in
sand (as Christ, see John 8); and some have written on glass
(as in the case of this hymn).

Its origin is very interesting and should be remembered. Miss
Harriet Auber, who lived the greater part of her life at Hoddesdon in Herts., had come back from Church on Whit-Sunday

morning and was thinking over what she had heard in the sermon. It appears that a sudden afflatus, or inspiration, came upon her, and this hymn was in her mind. Being eager to set it down before it had gone from her, and not finding paper handy, she slipped her diamond ring from her finger and wrote it on one of the panes of glass in the window. Afterwards it was transcribed to paper and appeared in print in 1829 in her collection entitled " The Spirit of the Psalms." It quickly passed into common use and was a favourite with C. H. Spurgeon, who included it in his hymn book.

One of Miss Auber's contemporaries, Mrs. Cuthbert Hadden, told the story in *The Young Woman* (1894). After her death, a dealer in curios tried to purchase this unusual manuscript, but without success. Soon afterwards it was stolen! It was cut out from its place, removed and its whereabouts lost in oblivion. But we have the hymn, and that is the main thing.

Not very much is known of Miss Auber. She was born in London on 4th October, 1773, and died at her home in Hoddesdon on 20th January, 1862. She was buried in the Churchyard of the Parish Church, where for so long she lived. She came to live in Hoddesdon when quite young, and spent the rest of her long life there. She lived to the great age of 89.

During her long life she wrote much poetry, most of which was of a devotional character. Her name first came into prominence when her " Spirit of the Psalms " was published in 1829. Julian tells us that several of her renderings of the Psalms are full of gentle melody and follow the evangelical interpretation of the Psalter. Psalm 73, " Whom have we, Lord, in Heaven but Thee," is very beautiful.

The hymn before us appeared with a second as suitable for Whit-Sunday, the day in the Church year on which it was written. It originally had seven stanzas, two of which are now usually omitted. One of them is specially good and its omission would appear to be a mistake. In case some do not know it, I will set it down:

> "He came in tongues of Living Flame,
>   To teach, convince, subdue;
> All powerful as the wind He came—
>   As viewless, too."

It is interesting to remember that this hymn has found its way into many lands and has been very widely translated. In the mission field when a new hymn book is being drawn up it is very unusual if this one is omitted. It appeals to simple minds and yet its profundities are like those of Pentecost. It is a favourite with children, and when one asks them about Pentecost and the Holy Spirit it is often quoted. It is really a metrical version of Acts 2.

It is an amazingly quiet hymn and is almost always sung to the tune St. Cuthbert. Indeed, one cannot remember it being sung to any other tune. It is probably true to say that the tune has helped to make the hymn so widely known, though it would have lived as a poem if never sung.

This tune was written by Dr. J. B. Dykes, the Vicar of St. Oswald's, Durham, who wrote about 300 hymn tunes. On Sunday evenings after the evening service, his own family and a few friends would gather and go over these tunes, seeking to improve and adapt them.

As we have already seen, the hymn is all about Pentecost, and is full of tenderness and quiet. It describes the work of the Holy Spirit and at the same time extols and exalts the Redeemer.

The Name of the Holy Spirit in the Upper Room discourse is " The Comforter," and this name is used in verse 1. It means literally " the One who makes strong by His Presence." With His advocacy the weak are brave again and arms are strong.

Next we see Him as the guest coming in Christ's name to indwell His people. It is important to grasp that He exercised an influence rather than being that influence. The Holy Spirit is a Person, not an influence, though as with every person He makes His Presence felt.

Then the Voice. The great American preacher, Theodore Parker, had a memorable experience as a young man, which he never forgot. He picked up a stone to throw at a turtle that was basking in the sun, and as he did so, he heard one word, " Stop!" He raced home and told his mother, who said it must have been the Voice of the Holy Spirit. " He checks each thought!"

Note in verse 4 the word " every." It occurs three times. Frances Ridley Havergal used to say: " All that is good in me is due to the Holy Spirit, all that is bad is due to myself."

We end on the note of prayer, and this is always the right response in His Presence.

From Greenland's icy mountains

REGINALD HEBER
1783-1826

From Greenland's icy mountains,
  From India's coral strand,
Where Afric's sunny fountains
  Roll down their golden sand;
From many an ancient river,
  From many a palmy plain,
They call us to deliver
  Their land from error's chain.

What though the spicy breezes
  Blow soft o'er Ceylon's isle,
Though every prospect pleases,
  And only man is vile:
In vain with lavish kindness
  The gifts of God are strown,
The heathen in his blindness
  Bows down to wood and stone.

Can we, whose souls are lighted
  With wisdom from on high,
Can we to men benighted
  The lamp of life deny?
Salvation, O salvation!
  The joyful sound proclaim,
Till each remotest nation
  Has learnt Messiah's name.

Waft, waft, ye winds, His story,
  And you, ye waters, roll;
Till, like a sea of glory,
  It spreads from pole to pole;
Till, o'er our ransom'd nature,
  The Lamb for sinners slain,
Redeemer, King, Creator,
  In bliss returns to reign.

OTHER HYMNS BY REGINALD HEBER:

Holy, Holy, Holy, Lord God Almighty.
The Son of God Goes Forth to War.
Brightest and Best of the Sons of the Morning.

TUNES: *Aurelia.*
        Greenland.

IT is sometimes forgotten in these days when the number of hymns is so vast that, 100 years ago, the choice was very limited, perhaps particularly on the missionary side. There were not a large number of missionary hymns. The first book of specifically missionary hymns was the *Church Missionary Hymn Book*, which first came out in 1899. Previous to this of course there had been sheets of missionary hymns.

If we put ourselves back into the lifetime of Reginald Heber, or even to the date of his Home-call in 1826, we can imagine how things stood.' I have introduced our hymn in this way because I think it will explain its origin possibly better than anything else.

Perhaps the speed with which the hymn was written is as remarkable as its origin. It was produced in its present form in the short space of 20 minutes. This reflects something of the spirituality of the man, of his close walk with God; it also reveals his deep missionary interest which later bore fruit when he became a missionary Bishop; it also reminds us of his great poetical ability, recalling the fact that when he was at Oxford he won the coveted Newdigate Prize for the best poem of the year.

On the Saturday before Whit-Sunday, 1819, Reginald Heber, who was then Vicar of Hodnet, near Crewe, was staying at Wrexham with his father-in-law, Dr. Shipley, Dean of St. Asaph. The next day the good Doctor was to preach a missionary sermon on behalf of the Society for the Propagation of the Gospel in Foreign Parts, and asked Heber to write a hymn which could be sung as an appropriate climax to the service. At once he set about his task and in two or three minutes had the first three verses ready of " From Greenland's Icy Mountains," which were a kind of outpost of missions at that time. The Dean thought these three verses sufficient, but Heber was not satisfied, and sat down again and completed the hymn. " Waft, waft, ye winds, His story . . . " Were twenty minutes ever better spent?

Reginald Heber was the distinguished son of a noble father, who himself was a Fellow of Brasenose College at Oxford. He was born at Malpas in Cheshire in 1783, and when only 17, entered his father's College, where he had a brilliant career. His Newdigate poem on " Palestine " is one of the few prize poems that have lived.

For 16 years he was Vicar of Hodnet, where he combined the two positions of pastor and squire. Thackeray's tribute in *The Four Georges* will never be forgotten. He mentions Collingwood as a good man of letters and Heber as a type of a good divine. Thackeray's paragraph has become almost proverbial:

" The charming poet, the happy possessor of all sorts of gifts and accomplishments — birth, wit, fame, high character, competence — he was the beloved priest in his own home of Hodnet, counselling the people in their trouble, advising them in their difficulties, kneeling often at their sick beds at the hazard of his own life; where there was strife, the peacemaker; where there was want, the free giver."

From the first, right on to the end when he laid down his life after a short episcopate in India, he was a person of great courage. When a boy, the doctor proposed to bleed him for whooping cough. His nurse protested, but the little sufferer settled it with these words: " Send poor nurse downstairs, I won't stir. Don't hold me." And he held out his arm for the lancet.

When offered the Bishopric of Calcutta for the second time, he felt it was God's call, and he could not refuse. It was a large diocese including Ceylon as well as the whole of India. After three short years filled to the full with apostolic labours and devotion, years of advance in every direction, he died at Trichinopoly at the early age of 43. On April 3rd, 1826, he confirmed 42 persons, and although deeply moved by the work going on in the struggling mission, he showed no signs of bodily exhaustion. On his return from the service he retired into his own room, and according to his invariable custom, wrote on the back of the address on Confirmation " Trichinopoly, April 3rd, 1826." This was his last act, for immediately on taking off his clothes, he went into a large cold bath, where he had bathed the two preceding mornings, but which was now the destined agent of his removal to Paradise. Half an hour after, his servant, alarmed at his long absence, entered the room and found his lifeless body.

This hymn is so well known that no comment is needed on it, but I want to point out its biblical origin. It is based on a passage in the Acts: 16: 6-15.

6. Now when Paul and Timothy had gone throughout

Phrygia and the region of Galatia, and were forbidden of the
Holy Ghost to preach the word in Asia.

7. After they were come to Mysia, they assayed to go into
Bithynia; but the Spirit suffered them not.

8. And they passing by Mysia came down to Troas.

9. And a vision appeared to Paul in the night. There stood
a man of Macedonia, and prayed him, saying, Come over into
Macedonia, and help us.

10. And after he had seen the vision, immediately we en-
deavoured to go into Macedonia, assuredly gathering that the
Lord had called us for to preach the gospel unto them.

11. Therefore loosing from Troas, we came with a straight
course to Samothracia, and the next day to Neapolis.

12. And from thence to Philippi, which is the chief city of
that part of Macedonia, and a colony; and we were in that city
abiding certain days.

13. And on the sabbath we went out of the city by a river
side, where prayer was wont to be made; and we sat down, and
spake unto the women which resorted thither.

14. And a certain woman named Lydia, a seller of purple,
of the city of Thyatira, which worshipped God heard us; whose
heart the Lord opened, that she attended unto the things which
were spoken of Paul.

15. And when she was baptized, and her household, she
besought us, saying, If ye have judged me to be faithful to the
Lord, come into my house, and abide there. And she constrained
us.

O Worship the King

SIR ROBERT GRANT
1779-1838

O worship the King, all glorious above;
    O gratefully sing His power and His love,
Our Shield and Defender, the Ancient of days,
    Pavilion'd in splendour, and girded with praise.

O tell of His might, O sing of His grace,
    Whose robe is the light; whose canopy space;
His chariots of wrath the deep thunder-clouds form,
    And dark is His path on the wings of the storm.

The earth, with its store of wonders untold,
    Almighty, Thy power hath founded of old,
Hath stablish'd it fast by a changeless decree,
    And round it hath cast, like a mantle, the sea.

Thy bountiful care what tongue can recite?
    It breathes in the air, it shines in the light;
It streams from the hills, it descends to the plain,
    And sweetly distils in the dew and the rain.

Frail children of dust, and feeble as frail,
    In Thee do we trust, nor find Thee to fail:
Thy mercies how tender, how firm to the end,
    Our Maker, Defender, Redeemer, and Friend.

O measureless Might, ineffable Love,
    While angels delight to hymn Thee above,
The humbler creation, though feeble their lays,
    With true adoration shall sing to Thy praise.

OTHER HYMNS BY SIR ROBERT GRANT:

Saviour, When in Dust to Thee.
When Gathering Clouds Around I View.

TUNES: *Hanover.*
Houghton.

IT is remarkable how few hymns, speaking comparatively, have been written by laymen. By far the greatest majority were composed by Ministers of the Gospel in the various denominations, greatly varying. I am going to venture to pick out three laymen and three laywomen whose work ranks with the very highest in the other category:

Charlotte Elliott — *Just as I am, without one plea.*

Frances Alexander — *There is a green hill far away.*

Fanny Crosby — *To God be the glory, great things He hath done.*

James Montgomery — *Hail to the Lord's anointed.*

James Edmeston — *Lead us, Heavenly Father, lead us.*

Robert Grant — *O Worship the King.*

C

You will see that I have included Robert Grant in my list, and so if I am right, we can consider him among our greatest hymn writers. I think it is true to say that no hymn is more popular than this. It suits almost any great occasion and is particularly suitable in the spring and at autumn time.

Those who are familiar with George Smith's *XII Indian Statesmen* will know how he epitomizes Robert's father, Charles Grant. He calls him " the first and greatest of Indian philanthropists." The list of his achievements is a very long one. He purged the East India Company's Government of abuses . . . he sent out evangelical chaplains through Simeon . . . he founded Haileybury College . . . he was a chief agent in the foundation of the C.M.S. and British and Foreign Bible Society, he fought for freedom of the African slave . . . etc., etc. But Robert had a noble brother as well as a noble father, whose name was Charles, afterwards Lord Glenelg, who afterwards collected his brother Robert's verses under the title " Sacred Poems." Lord Brougham pronounced Lord Glenelg " the purest statesman he had ever known."

Belonging to such a family, we are not surprised that Robert Grant became the man he did. He graduated from Cambridge in 1806, being called to the Bar the following year, and becoming M.P. for Inverness in 1826, and a Privy Councillor in 1834. In the same year he was appointed Governor of Bombay, but he only held the position for four years, dying at Dapoorie in Western India on 9th July, 1938. Thus a great career was cut short very early.

At a public meeting of the inhabitants of Bombay, to arrange for a tribute to his memory, striking testimony was made to his great work as Governor and to his noble Christian character. A medical college bearing his name was built to commemorate him, and it stands to this day. In addition a street in Bombay was named after him, and one is led to understand that such a move in India is a very high honour. It is a very stirring thing to recall the deep spiritual character of the man whose hymn is now to be touched on. " These hymns show that there was in the heart of their author a rich vein of spiritual life," writes one admirer.

Grant's hymns were written at different periods of his life, as the Spirit moved him, and appeared in periodicals like the

Christian Observer. They were printed under the signature, "E . . . . . 7, D.R."

A very precious meditation is possible if Genesis 1, Psalm 104, and " O Worship the King " are read together. It will be quickly seen that the hymn is a metrical commentary on the six days of creation. Let me try and make a comparison:

DAY 1. LIGHT.
O tell of His might, O sing of His grace,
Whose robe is the light

DAY 2. AIR AND WATER.
And dark is His path on the wings of the storm.

DAY 3. LAND AND SEA.
The earth, with its store . . .
And round it hath cast, like a mantle, the sea.

DAY 4. LIGHTS.
It breathes in the air, it shines in the light;

DAY 5. FOWL AND FISH.
The humbler creation, though feeble their lays.

DAY 6. MAN.
Frail children of dust, and feeble as frail,
In Thee do we trust,

O WORSHIP THE KING.
One of the merits of the hymn is the prominence it gives to God, and the various aspects of His character which are brought into view by the cluster of God's names, all of which ought to be dwelt on and pondered in the light of Holy Scripture. I cannot do more than give a list of them with appropriate texts attached:

King	Psalm 10: 16.
Shield	Psalm 28: 7.
Defender	Psalm 59: 9.
Ancient of Days	Daniel 7: 13.
Maker	Psalm 95: 6.
Redeemer	Job 19: 25.
Friend	Proverbs 18: 24.

Just as I am, without one plea

CHARLOTTE ELLIOTT
1789-1871

Just as I am — without one plea,
But that Thy blood was shed for me,
And that Thou bidd'st me come to Thee —
 O Lamb of God, I come.

Just as I am — and waiting not
To rid my soul of one dark blot,
To Thee, whose blood can cleanse each spot —
 O Lamb of God, I come.

Just as I am — though toss'd about
With many a conflict, many a doubt,
Fightings and fears within, without —
 O Lamb of God, I come.

Just as I am — poor, wretched, blind;
Sight, riches, healing of the mind,
Yea, all I need, in Thee to find —
 O Lamb of God, I come.

Just as I am — Thou wilt receive,
Wilt welcome, pardon, cleanse, relieve,
Because Thy promise I believe —
 O Lamb of God, I come.

Just as I am — Thy love unknown
Has broken every barrier down;
Now, to be Thine, yea, Thine alone —
 O Lamb of God, I come.

Just as I am — of that free love
The breadth, length, depth, and height to prove,
Here for a season, then above —
 O Lamb of God, I come.

OTHER HYMNS BY CHARLOTTE ELLIOTT:

Christian Seek Not Yet Repose.
My God My Father While I Stray.

TUNES: *Misericordia.*
Saffron Walden.

CHARLOTTE ELLIOTT, whose hymn, "Just as I am," is to be the subject of this chapter, was born in Clapham in 1789, the year of the French Revolution. This village, three miles out of London, with its 1,000 inhabitants, was the home of numerous prominent Christians at that time. There was Charles Grant, Chairman of the East India Company; Lord Teignmouth, former Governor of India; Henry Thornton, a wealthy merchant; James Stephen, the lawyer; and William Wilberforce, court favourite, Parliamentary orator, and liberator of the slaves.

They were all members of the National Church and derived their inspiration from its Prayer Book and from the ministry of a godly Vicar, John Venn, a member of a distinguished family bearing that name. Charlotte Elliott attended the same Church and heard Venn's gospel preaching, but it meant little to her. Family worship in her home left her cold. She tells how fond she was of sacred music, but it did not reach her heart. Although thoughtful and wistful, she did not have the assurance and joy which she saw in her relatives. Gradually she grew apathetic.

The crisis in her experience came in 1822 when she was just over 30. A distinguished guest came to her home at Grove House that year — Dr. Caesar Malan, a minister from Geneva. He quickly noticed this young woman who seemed so much *in* things socially, and yet so much *out* of things when it came to spiritual realities. Dr. Malan determined to speak to her, although personal approaches of this kind were not much in vogue then. Soon the opportunity came. Begging her to confide in him, he asked whether she were a Christian. The young lady was deeply offended; she drew herself up to her full height, threw back her head, and asked the visitor if in future he would mind his own business. Dr. Malan apologised, and promised to pray for her.

But Charlotte could not dismiss that question from her mind: Was she a Christian? That conversation remained in her memory and troubled her for many a long day. A fortnight later, she and Dr. Malan chanced, no doubt providentially, to find themselves in the garden together, and began to talk to each other. Apologising for her rudeness, Charlotte said she had been thinking a good deal about his question. "I should like to come to Christ," she said, "but I don't know how." "My dear young lady," Dr. Malan replied, putting his hand on her shoulder, " you need worry no more about that, come to Him just as you are."

That talk and those words led to the birth of a soul, and the birth of a song.

Let us go forward 12 years. The family has moved from Clapham to Brighton, where Charlotte's brother is Vicar. At this time Mr. Elliott was very busy establishing a school for the daughters of clergymen. But Charlotte could have no share whatever in this vigorous labour of love; she was weak and ill and unable to help. Steadily she became more and more depressed. Why could she do nothing when so much needed to be done? Why was she a burden when she wanted to be such a help? Had God forsaken her? Was she a castaway? It was all so disappointing and naturally she was increasingly downcast.

It was at this critical juncture that Dr. Malan's words came back to her mind: " Come to Him as you are." Then she went back in thought to the starting point, and peace returned to her troubled heart. Suddenly she was filled with a strong emotion and felt the desire to express her jubilation in words. Quickly taking up her pen, she wrote down these lovely verses, as if borne along by a divine impulse:

> " Just as I am, though tossed about
>   With many a conflict, many a doubt;
>   Fighting and fears, within, without,
>   O Lamb of God, I come."

At first the hymn was published anonymously and was widely circulated. One friend, thinking it would be a blessing to Charlotte, sent it to her, never imagining that it was her composition.

This hymn has been owned by God in a remarkable way and used to comfort many. After Charlotte Elliott's death, a box was found among her possessions which contained over 1,000 letters telling of spiritual help received through the hymn. This hymn was used more than any other in Moody's meetings in this country. If translation is a criterion of literary excellence (and many think it is), then this hymn must be given a high place in any list of great hymns. It has been translated into almost every language, and is sung on every continent.

When the poet Wordsworth's daughter was suffering during her last illness, someone sent her a copy of this hymn, and we are not surprised to learn that she was comforted on her death bed. As it was read over in her presence she exclaimed, " Why, that is the very thing for me." Sometimes she asked for it as many as ten times a day. It may well be that her father, the Poet Laureate, read it to her sometimes. It is striking that when Wordsworth was laid to rest in Grasmere Churchyard and a memorial was erected over the grave, a lamb with a cross behind it was carved on the stone. Underneath there is the inscription, " Him that cometh unto Me, I will in no wise cast out."

That was Dora Wordsworth's text; it was also Charlotte Elliott's. These are the very words she wrote as a heading for her hymn in the original draft in 1834:

> " Just as I am without one plea
> But that Thy blood was shed for me,
> And that Thou bidst me come to Thee,
> O Lamb of God, I come."

But I must end on a personal note: Can I come to Christ like this? Can I come to Him just as I am? Turning to the Gospels we get our answer: The leper came to Jesus just as he was—a poor leper; the blind man was brought to Jesus, groping in the darkness, just as he was; with the palsied man it was just the same; the boy suffering from epilepsy came just as he was; the sinful woman of Samaria could not cleanse herself, so she came to Jesus just as she was.

A man once said to Moody: " I feel as if I am chained, I cannot come to Christ." " Come, chains and all," said the great evangelist. " Come just as you are — Christ can deliver you — only come!"

> " Just as I am — Thou wilt receive,
> Wilt welcome, pardon, cleanse, relieve;
> Because Thy promise I believe —
> O Lamb of God, I come."

Lead us, heavenly father, lead us

JAMES EDMESTON
1791-1867

Lead us, heavenly Father, lead us
 O'er the world's tempestuous sea;
Guard us, guide us, keep us, feed us,
 For we have no help but Thee;
  Yet possessing
  Every blessing,
 If our God our Father be.

Saviour, breathe forgiveness o'er us;
 All our weakness Thou dost know;
Thou didst tread this earth before us,
 Thou didst feel its keenest woe;
  Lone and dreary,
  Faint and weary,
 Through the desert Thou didst go.

Spirit of our God, descending,
 Fill our hearts with heavenly joy;
Love with every passion blending,
 Pleasure that can never cloy:
  Thus provided,
  Pardon'd, guided,
 Nothing can our peace destroy.

OTHER HYMNS BY JAMES EDMESTON:

Little Travellers Zionwards.
Saviour Breathe an Evening Blessing.

TUNE: *Mannheim.*

THIS hymn has been in regular use for nearly 100 years, and
 is very frequently sung. Although appearing first in 1821, it
was not widely known until 1858, when it was included in
" Baptist Psalms and Hymns." Since then it has grown in favour
and Julian claims that " it has attained to a foremost place
amongst modern hymns in all English-speaking countries."

In 1821 Edmeston included it in his " Sacred Lyrics," and
entitled it, " Hymn, Written for the Children of the London
Orphan Asylum." Unlike many hymns which have been altered

either more or less, from the start this one has been considered as nearly perfect as possible. It is an invocation of the Trinity and yet the language is of the simplest and the emphasis very practical. It is a hymn much in use at weddings, doubtless because it expresses the aspirations of so many young couples.

To whatever hymn book we turn this hymn is printed without any verbal alteration, which I always feel is about the highest compliment we can pay to a hymn writer. Some hymns have been so seriously amended that the character of the hymn has been altered from the original.

James Edmeston was born 10th September, 1791, in London. His grandfather was Pastor of an Independent Church at Stepney for 50 years. Trained as an architect and surveyor, he set up on his own account in 1816, and continued in practice until his death on 7th January, 1867. One of his pupils was the famous Sir Gilbert Scott, some of whose work is so beautiful. Perhaps I may single out for all lovers of the Reformation the Martyrs' Memorial in St. Giles Street at Oxford. " Painfully beautiful," was the exclamation of the man who hoped to get the job, and then uttered the challenge that no one could put up anything worthy of Oxford.

Although an Independent by descent, Edmeston joined the Church of England in early life and was a devoted adherent. At one time he was Churchwarden at St. Barnabas, Homerton.

Many of his 2,000 hymns were for children, and there are many lovely stories about many of them. " Little Travellers Zionwards " was contributed to a missionary magazine edited by Mrs. Luke, the authoress of " I think, when I read that sweet story of old." When she received these lovely lines she was overwhelmed; they " brought a rush of tears to my eyes, and I acknowledged them with no stinted praise."

His best known hymn but one, " Saviour, Breathe an Evening Blessing," was suggested by a scene described in Saltes' " Travels in Abyssinia at Night." The writer describes how the singing of an evening hymn brought peace to all as night fell, stealing upon every ear in camp. The idea of safe-keeping comes into this lovely hymn and it was very much needed.

> " Though destruction walk around us,
>   Though the arrow past us fly;
> Angel guards from Thee surround us
>   We are safe if Thou art nigh."

It seems a pity that more of his beautiful children's hymns cannot be revived. They are still amazingly fresh and full of Scriptural allusions. One feels that Edmeston is a hymn writer whose work has been much overlooked and whose merits have not been appreciated as they should.

As I have said already, this hymn is an invocation to the Trinity, each verse referring to one of the Persons in this order, Father, Son, Holy Ghost. This is how we can sum up the verses. The Father as the source of every blessing, without whom we are helpless; the Son as our great Exemplar without whom we are friendless; the Holy Ghost descending, in the Son's name, without whom we are joyless.

We might take up the thoughts here in prayer and say, " Father, keep us in Thy way: Jesus, breathe forgiveness o'er us: Holy Spirit, fill us with joy." We note that life is a storm, a journey, a battle, and our need is for God, Father, Son and Holy Ghost. Guidance, forgiveness, joy, such is God's provision for us. In each verse prayer is made to the Person of the Trinity addressed: " Keep us," " Forgive us," " Fill us."

One loves the vision of Christ which we get in verse 2. He set His face like a flint to endure all that was appointed for Him to bear. We have not an High Priest which cannot be touched with the feeling of our infirmities, but was in all points tempted like as we, yet without sin.

Some hymns seem to bring God very near and make Him very precious. This is one of them in a special sense. " God is in this place," we say, " and I knew it not." Whenever we sing this hymn may its prayerful aspirations all be fulfilled in individual cases.

Ride on, ride on, in Majesty

HENRY HART MILMAN
1791-1868

Ride on, ride on in majesty;
  Hark! all the tribes Hosanna cry:
O Saviour meek, pursue Thy road,
  With palms and scatter'd garments strow'd.

Ride on, ride on in majesty;
    In lowly pomp ride on to die:
O Christ, Thy triumphs now begin
    O'er captive death and conquer'd sin.

Ride on, ride on in majesty;
    The wingèd squadrons of the sky
Look down with sad and wondering eyes
    To see the approaching sacrifice.

Ride on, ride on in majesty;
    Thy last and fiercest strife is nigh:
The Father on His sapphire throne
    Expects His own anointed Son.

Ride on, ride on in majesty;
    In lowly pomp ride on to die:
Bow Thy meek head to mortal pain;
    Then take, O God, Thy power, and reign.

OTHER HYMNS BY HENRY HART MILMAN:
    Bound Upon the Accursed Tree.
    When Our Heads are Bowed with Woe.
    O Help Us, Lord! Each Hour of Need.

TUNES: *St. Drostane.*
            Winchester New.

SOME of our hymns are definitely associated with certain of the Church seasons. The one before us is one of the great Palm Sunday hymns. Julian calls it one of the best for this particular day. Most of Milman's thirteen hymns, all of which are in common use, were written for use in connection with one of the Sundays in the Church Calendar. For instance, "When our heads are bowed with woe" for Lent II; and "Bound upon the Accursed Tree" for Good Friday — and let us not forget that the title of that day, "Good Friday," came into use at the time of the Reformation, when the message of the finished work of Christ again came into prominence, after being out of sight for several centuries, during the time we call "the Dark Ages."

These hymns arose from the suggestion of his friend, Bishop Reginald Heber, whose episcopate of apostolic zeal at Calcutta has been immortalised in the Life by George Smith. Heber, Milman's "early friend," decided to arrange a series of hymns for the Christian Year, and decided to appeal to Milman for help, as well as to others. When " Ride on, Ride on in Majesty " was sent to him by Milman, he wrote, " a few more such hymns and I shall neither need nor wait for the aid of Scott and Southey." Heber's volume of hymns which first appeared in 1812 was re-issued in 1827, and included Milman's thirteen hymns, which we thus see were all written in early life. Heber contributed " From Greenland's Icy Mountains," "' Holy, Holy, Holy," " The Son of God Goes Forth to War," and others.

In spite of Milman's great promise as a scholar and preacher in later years, it is safe to say that his name will be perpetuated by his hymns. One is bound to say that out of 99 who know of his hymns only one will have heard of his " History of the Jews " or his " History of Latin Christianity." His best known hymn is the one we are looking at, but not far behind is " When Our Heads are Bowed with Woe." Julian says, " This hymn has no peer in its presentation of Christ's human sympathy." A hymn more full of deep consolation it would be difficult to find:

> " When the heart is sad within,
> With the thought of all its sin;
> When the spirit shrinks with fear,
> Gracious Son of Mary, hear!
>
> Thou the same, the grief, has known,
> Though the sins were not Thine own;
> Thou has deigned their load to bear;
> Gracious Son of Mary, hear."

Henry Hart Milman, the youngest son of Sir Francis Milman, Physician to George III, was born in London in 1791. From Dr. Burney's School at Greenwich he went to Eton and then to Brasenose College, Oxford, where he had a brilliant career. Ordained in 1816, he was soon appointed Vicar of Reading. He was made Professor of Poetry in 1821 and ten years later was followed by John Keble. In 1827 he delivered the famous Bampton Lectures. Sir Robert Peel presented him to a Canonry at Westminster in 1835 and the Rectory of St. Margaret's; and in 1849 he became Dean of St. Paul's on the nomination of Lord John Russell, a position which he held till his death in 1868. Some of his greatest work was done at St. Paul's, where he introduced popular Sunday evening services. No greater man than Dean Milman — poet, scholar, historian — has ever filled that important office in the Church.

All through his life he poured out a continual flow of literature of one sort and another, and his pen was never idle. It is impossible even to enumerate his many writings, some of which are masterpieces in their own field.

Of his early poetical works " The Tragedy of Fazio " is most worth reading, but all of them are polished and deeply stirring. His greatest prose achievement is " A History of Latin Christianity Down to the Death of Pope Nicholas V (1855)." His Bampton Lectures on " The Character of the Apostles as an Evidence of Christianity " is still full of life, and when I once consulted it I found it most gripping. His sentences and paragraphs are often long and complicated, but the reader's compensation comes in the discovery of unforgettable epigrams and antitheses.

The context of Milman's life can be seen if we remember that as a boy he witnessed the burial of Nelson at St. Paul's, and as its Dean officiated at the funeral of the Duke of Wellington.

This hymn should be read side by side with the Scripture account of Christ's entry into Jerusalem. Take St. John 12: 12-19. You will find that if both are read together the hymn will greatly help you to realize that remarkable scene when Christ fulfilled the prophecy in Zechariah, and rode into Jerusalem upon an ass. It was a ride characterized by majesty and humility, and Milman captures both elements.

The first verse shows us Christ on the road from Bethany to Jerusalem, riding upon the ass which the disciples had brought from the village over against them. We see the branches of the palm trees and the garments laid carefully on the road to make a carpet for the King.

In verse two, the purpose of it all is brought before us. It is to die that He comes. This road leads to sacrifice, but sacrifice is never alone. It ushers in victory, victory here over sin and death, both of which were mighty conquerors.

In the third verse the angels are introduced, angels who sang at his birth over the fields of nearby Bethlehem and now look down in wonder. No singing yet! The passage of Scripture which comes to mind is 1 Peter 1: 11-12: " . . . the sufferings of Christ . . . which things the angels desire to look into."

They wondered and enquired as they saw the approaching sacrifice, but could not fathom its significance.

When we come to verse 4, we pass into the Father's presence. God the Father whose holy will is going to be done to the full by the willing victim, waits for His beloved Son. It must have encouraged Jesus to know that the Father approved every step and that there was a matchless welcome ahead.

At the end, the thought recurs of His death leading to triumph. What looked like a disaster was a deliverance. Christ triumphed over His enemy and ours and robbed him of his spoils. In some manuscripts of the Septuagint, Psalm 96: 10 runs, " The Lord reigned from the tree! " This is the thought in the hymn. Not only was He King of the Jews as the inscription stated, but King of all, as the three languages, Greek, Hebrew and Latin hinted.

Abide with me! fast falls the eventide

HENRY FRANCIS LYTE
1793-1847

Abide with me: fast falls the eventide;
   The darkness deepens; Lord, with me abide:
When other helpers fail, and comforts flee,
   Help of the helpless, O, abide with me.

Swift to its close ebbs out life's little day;
   Earth's joys grow dim, its glories pass away;
Change and decay in all around I see;
   O Thou, who changest not, abide with me.

Come not in terrors, as the King of kings;
   But kind and good, with healing in Thy wings;
Tears for all woes, a heart for every plea;
   Come, Friend of sinners, thus abide with me.

I need Thy presence every passing hour:
   What but Thy grace can foil the tempter's power?
Who like Thyself my guide and stay can be?
   Through cloud and sunshine, O, abide with me.

I fear no foe, with Thee at hand to bless:
    Ills have no weight, and tears no bitterness:
Where is death's sting? where, grave, thy victory?
    I triumph still, if Thou abide with me.

Hold Thou Thy cross before my closing eyes;
    Shine through the gloom, and point me to the skies;
Heaven's morning breaks, and earth's vain shadows flee;
    In life, in death, O Lord, abide with me.

OTHER HYMNS BY HENRY F. LYTE:
Pleasant Are Thy Courts Above.
Praise My Soul, the King of Heaven.

TUNE: *Eventide.*

As one stands on the quay at Brixham in South Devon, it is so quiet and peaceful that you would never think it had been the scene of many eventful happenings. It was from there that the men of Devon pushed off to meet the Spanish Armada in 1588; it was on to this spot that William of Orange stepped to re-establish Protestantism in 1688; it was in the bay that the " Bellerophon " anchored — the ship that carried Napoleon to St. Helena; it was there that one of our greatest hymns first saw the light.

It is scarcely necessary to speak of the popularity of this hymn. On November 16th, 1947, when a memorial to Lyte's memory was unveiled in Westminster Abbey and the hymn was sung, the crowd outside took it up; sixty years ago when the *Sunday at Home* asked for a list of 100 best hymns, this one was second on the list; some years back when Sir F. J. Wall, the Secretary of the Football Association, was drawing up the programme for the Cup Final, he ran his pen through " Alexander's Ragtime Band " and inserted this hymn.

This hymn has sustained men in the hour of spiritual crisis, as at Dunkirk; it has cheered men in their labours, as the fishermen at Brixham are cheered by the chimes of their Church at eight o'clock every night; it has helped folk to face death, for instance, Nurse Cavell; it has comforted men in trials, for example, the long wait which Gordon had at Khartoum.

Henry Lyte, the child of English parents, was born in 1793 in Scotland, and subsequently educated in Ireland. He died of consumption on November 20th, 1847, at Nice, in the South of France.

In the year 1815 he was ordained and began his life work as a Curate at Taghmon in County Wexford. Some five years later he returned there for a holiday and heard of the illness of an old friend, William le Hunte. The dying man was haunted by the thought that he would lose the sense of the Lord's presence which he enjoyed, and exclaimed, " O, abide with me, abide with me!" Was that the first inspiration for the hymn?

At this time he was Curate of Marazion in Cornwall. It was while there that he had an experience which changed his whole outlook. A clergyman who was dying, appealed to Lyte for spiritual help which he could not give. They then began to study the Bible together and were both led to see in Christ the only One who could deal with their sin!

In 1823 he was appointed to Brixham, where he remained till his death 24 years later. There he kept his congregation under a sacred spell, and his theme was ever " The redeeming power of Christ's sacrifice on the Cross of Calvary." Every ship that came into port he provided with a Bible.

Late in the summer of 1847 he was very ill, and his family was surprised when he announced that before leaving home he would preach a farewell sermon, following the Lord's Supper. That afternoon, September 5th, he rested, then took a quiet walk; in the evening he handed a manuscript to his daugher — the hymn which we are looking at now, which he called " a dying man's legacy to his family and the world."

When we look at the hymn we notice that the theme is the need for Christ's presence. The Christ who once was dead is now alive and needed by all for a number of reasons. These are some: We need Him because the eventide of life is sure to come. " Hold Thou Thy Cross before my closing eyes." What an appeal this hymn makes to those whose days on earth are numbered! Every minister who has sung it at the bedside knows full well.

We need Him because men are what they are. It is said that not long before this hymn was written a number of men had left his choir. When other helpers fail! We are all disappointing to one another, so the need of Christ is insistent.

We need Him because we live in a changing world; we need a Rock and an anchor. Change and decay in all around I see. There's One who changes not; upon Him we can lean.

We need Him because in youth we must learn to walk with

Christ if we are to be kept from falling. Some lines which do not usually appear in our collections are full of interest:

> " Thou on my head in early youth didst smile,
> And, though rebellious and perverse meanwhile,
> Thou hast not left me, oft as I left Thee,
> On to the close, O Lord, abide with me."

We need Him because trials are sure to come. We are told in " South " how great were the perils which Sir Ernest Shackleton had to face. One of his greatest inspirations was a gramophone record of this hymn sung by Dame Clara Butt. " O Thou who changest not, abide with me."

Lyte got his inspiration for this hymn from the story of Christ's walk to Emmaus with the two depressed disciples. " Abide with us " they prayed, and constrained Him to stay. The word means " compelled by force." Christ waits to be constrained. Have you compelled Him by force to come into your life?

Sun of my Soul, Thou Saviour dear

JOHN KEBLE
1792-1866

> Sun of my soul, Thou Saviour dear,
> It is not night if Thou be near;
> O may no earth-born cloud arise,
> To hide Thee from Thy servant's eyes.

> When the soft dews of kindly sleep
> My wearied eyelids gently steep,
> Be my last thought, how sweet to rest
> For ever on my Saviour's breast.

> Abide with me from morn till eve,
> For without Thee I cannot live;
> Abide with me when night is nigh,
> For without Thee I dare not die.

> If some poor wandering child of Thine
> Have spurn'd today the voice divine,
> Now, Lord, the gracious work begin;
> Let him no more lie down in sin.

Watch by the sick, enrich the poor
   With blessings from Thy boundless store;
Be every mourner's sleep tonight,
   Like infant's slumbers, pure and light.

Come near and bless us when we wake,
   Ere through the world our way we take,
Till in the ocean of Thy love
   We lose ourselves in heaven above.

OTHER HYMNS BY JOHN KEBLE:
   New Every Morning is the Love.
   The Voice that Breathed O'er Eden.
   There is a Book Who Runs May Read.

TUNES: *Abends.*
          Hursley.

A VISITOR at the home of Lord Tennyson asked him what he thought of Christ. The Poet Laureate was silent for a while as they continued to walk in the garden. Then he stopped, picked a flower, and said, " What the sun is to that flower, Jesus Christ is to my soul. He is the sun of my soul." John Keble felt this.

As the sunshine to the heavens,
   As the image to the glass,
As the fruit unto the fig tree,
   As the dew unto the grass.
     So, dear Lord, art Thou to me.

In the biography of John Ellerton by Henry Housman, we learn how William Wilberforce and his four sons planned a holiday together, each agreeing to bring a new book with them which could be read aloud to the party. When they disclosed their choice they each produced John Keble's " Christian Year."

It is in one of the poems that " Sun of my Soul " occurs. The " Christian Year " was composed as a companion to the Book of Common Prayer, and it is hardly too much to say that what the Prayer Book is in prose the " Christian Year " is in poetry. These poems were published in 1827 and yet they are for ever fresh and of abiding value.

Let us recall something of Keble's life and distinctions. He was born at the time of the French Revolution and he died at the age of 74 in 1866. He was coached by his father, a clergyman of the Vicarage of Coln St. Aldwyn in Gloucestershire, and won a scholarship to Corpus Christi College, Oxford, when only 15 years of age. He gained a Double First and won many other prizes. Keble was the second man to get two Firsts, Sir Robert Peel being the other. He was certainly one of the most outstanding undergraduates of his time.

He was ordained in 1815, the year of Waterloo, and served several curacies, one with his father, and he returned to Coln St. Aldwyn a second time to act again as his father's Curate while the old man recovered from a severe illness. When his father died in 1835, he was appointed to the living of Hursley, where he remained for 30 years. He was buried in Hursley Churchyard, and a short time afterwards his wife was laid to rest there too.

From 1831-1841 he was Professor of Poetry at Oxford and it was during this time that he gathered round him a small band of pupils of whom the most striking was Hurrell Froude, and in the circle organized the Tractarian Movement. In his sermon on National Apostasy (1833) Keble gave the signal for action, and for the next eight years was engaged with Newman, Pusey, Williams and others in the issue of " Tracts for the Times," brought to an end by " Tract 90 " in 1841. With Pusey he was the steadying influence in the group, especially under the shock caused by Newman's secession to Rome.

But the " Christian Year " is loved by Evangelicals as well as others. The late T. W. Drury used to deliver lectures at Ridley Hall upon it which were much appreciated.

It is correct to say that Keble was more of a poet than a hymn writer. The hymn before us was part of a much longer poem reaching to fourteen verses. The verses of the hymn were extracted by compilers rather than by Keble himself.

We should, therefore, study the context, and " Sun of My Soul " gains immensely in this way. The poem begins with a traveller overtaken by darkness and yet pushing on although the sun has set. The first two stanzas are as follows:

> 'Tis gone! that bright and orbèd blaze
> Fast fading from our wistful gaze;
> Yon mantling cloud has hid from sight
> The last faint pulse of quivering light.

> In darkness and in weariness
> The traveller on his way must press
> No gleam to watch in tree or bower
> Whiling away the lonesome hour.

Then comes our present hymn, " Sun of My Soul." In the darkness He is the one true light and He ever shines. The Sun of righteousness arises with healing in His wings. The poem has one verse which I like very much, it is for those set over us in authority.

> The Rulers of this Christian land,
> 'Twixt Thee and us ordained to stand —
> Guide Thou their course, O Lord aright,
> Let all do all as in Thy sight.

The quality of the poetry is such that it was wanted everywhere; in the 25 years after publication it went through 43 editions. His love of nature comes out in nearly every poem, and he looks at it with an anointed eye and sees in it the handiwork of One who doeth all things well. Bishop Wilberforce said of Keble, " He gave England's Church the learning of a deep divine, the love and trust of a loyal son, the labour of a devoted priest, and the pattern of a saint."

(1) The sun is the source of life and light and warmth. So is Christ. When the sun shines it scatters all the shadows. No clouds must dim the vision of Him who is the light of the world.

(2) What a lovely " pillow " prayer is. Our last thought must be of Him, and if it is then our first will be of Him. And our rest in Christ now will be realized by and by in a rest with Christ for ever.

(3) Both life and death alike are impossible without Christ, for life is empty and death is doom if He be not there. Abide with Me — the word harks back to the Emmaus cottage.

(4) " Lord bring the wanderers home, stay the power of sin." Welcome and cleansing are our two great needs. " The gracious work " must be done by Him.

(5) The sick, the poor, the mourner, the child — each is mentioned lovingly in turn and embraced in a comprehensive prayer. Tonight — it is an evening hymn and it leads to seek the peace which passes all understanding.

(6) The waking hour comes when the night is over and then too, " I need Thee, O! I need Thee." We have to face

the world, or rather pass through it, for we are pilgrims. We lose ourselves. Would it not be better to say we find ourselves? We shall never be lost in any sense. Even in the ocean of His love our individual indebtedness to Him will be precious to the Saviour.

Crown Him with many crowns

MATTHEW BRIDGES
1800-1894

Crown Him with many crowns,
The Lamb upon His throne;
Hark! how the heavenly anthem drowns
All music but its own:
Awake, my soul, and sing
Of Him who died for thee,
And hail Him as thy matchless King
Through all eternity.

Crown Him the Virgin's Son,
The God Incarnate born,
Whose conquering arm those trophies won
Which now His brow adorn;
The Shiloh long foretold,
The Branch of Jesse's stem;
The Shepherd King of Israel's fold,
The Babe of Bethlehem.

Crown Him the Lord of love,
Behold His hands and side,
Those wounds yet visible above
In beauty glorified:
No angel in the sky
Can fully bear that sight,
But downward bends his wondering eye
At mysteries so bright.

Crown Him the Lord of peace,
Whose power a sceptre sways
From pole to pole, that wars may cease,
And all be prayer and praise:
His reign shall know no end,
And round His piercèd feet
Fair flowers of Paradise extend
Their fragrance ever sweet.

Crown Him the Lord of years,
The Potentate of time,
Creator of the rolling spheres,
Ineffably sublime.
All hail, Redeemer, hail!
For Thou hast died for me:
Thy praise and glory shall not fail
Throughout eternity.

OTHER HYMNS BY MATTHEW BRIDGES:

Rise, Glorious Conqueror, Rise.
Head of the Hosts in Glory.

TUNE: *Diademata.*

THIS is one of the hymns which usually occurs in the section specially relating to Christ, particularly Christ in glory; His Intercession and Reign; His Kingdom, Present and Future; Jesus is King. To me it is one of the most majestic hymns we could sing. When sung to the tune Diademata (Crowns) it is a hymn which makes one's aspirations soar up to Him who sits on the throne crowned with many crowns. This is how the hymn was originally headed: " In capite eins diademata multa."

Not very much is known of Matthew Bridges. Perhaps the most outstanding thing is that he was one of that small group of men like John Henry Newman, Frederick Faber and Edward Caswell, who left the Church of England and joined the Church of Rome at the time of the Oxford Movement. This happened in 1847 when he was 47 years of age. In 1852 he published a volume of poems on " The Passion of Jesus," in which this hymn was included, and called by the author " The Song of the Seraphs."

He was born in Essex in 1800, being the youngest son of John Bridges of Wallington House, Surrey. An older brother was Charles Bridges, the author of many books, including an exposition of the 69th Psalm, of which C. H. Spurgeon says in his book on commentaries, " Worth its weight in gold!" That is high praise!

Obviously Matthew had an excellent brother in Charles, but the latter must have been sad about the secession.

How he spent the last 40 years of his life, and where, no one is able to tell us. It is one of those mysteries which we sometimes meet with. He may easily have got swallowed up in a great organisation as others have been.

Besides some prose works he wrote " Babbacombe," or " Visions of Memory " with other poems (1842); " Hymns of the Heart " (1848); and the " Passion of Jesus " (1852). From this onwards we lose sight of him. His hymns in common use are taken from the last two productions.

Another hymn sometimes attributed to him is " Lo, He comes, with clouds descending." This hymn is a close imitation of one by Charles Wesley. And the name of John Cennick is also associated with the hymn. Bridges' version was published in " Hymns of the Heart " in 1848.

The tune " Diademata " to which this hymn is usually sung was composed by G. J. Elvey, who took his music degree at Oxford and was organist at St. George's, Windsor, for 50 years. One of his deepest convictions was that noble hymns should be sung to fitting music and that all should harmonise with the buildings in which they were sung. His idea was that in a Cathedral a hymn should have a special tune which would fill the building.

Now the hymn before us fits into this category most perfectly. The hymn is a majestic one and the tune " Diademata " a tremendous one forbidding any alternative. All the stops can come out when we come to verse six.

Let me pick out a thought for each verse, shall I say the key thought, as it appears to me?

(1) A call to the Church to join the heavenly lays and hail Christ as the King of kings.

(2) The Babe of Bethlehem is God Incarnate come as the Saviour of the world.

(3) The Gospel is Christ, Christ who died and rose again victorious, Whose glories are now to be the theme of the Christian's song.

(4) He is the Prince of Peace and from Him all thoughts of peace proceed, and in Him all hopes of peace centre. He maketh wars to cease in all the earth.

(5) Finally after being acclaimed as " Lord of Life, Lord of Peace, Lord of Heaven," He is saluted as " Lord of Years." Time is in His hands. But amid this burst of universal acclamation the personal note is not forgotten:

> " All hail, Redeemer, hail!
> For Thou hast died for me : "

Immortal love, for ever full

JOHN GREENLEAF WHITTIER
1807-1892

Immortal love, for ever full,
 For ever flowing free,
For ever shared, for ever whole,
 A never-ebbing sea.

Our outward lips confess the Name
 All other names above;
Love only knoweth whence it came,
 And comprehendeth love.

We may not climb the heavenly steeps
 To bring the Lord Christ down;
In vain we search the lowest deeps,
 For Him no depths can drown.

But warm, sweet, tender, even yet
 A present help is He;
And faith has still its Olivet,
 And love its Galilee.

The healing of His seamless dress
 Is by our beds of pain;
We touch Him in life's throng and press,
 And we are whole again.

O Lord and Master of us all
 Whate'er our name or sign,
We own Thy sway, we hear Thy call,
 We test our lives by Thine.

Our thoughts lie open to Thy sight;
 And naked to Thy glance
Our secret sins are in the light
 Of Thy pure countenance.

Apart from Thee all gain is loss,
 All labour vainly done;
The solemn shadow of Thy cross
 Is better than the sun.

Alone, O Love ineffable,
 Thy saving name is given,
To turn aside from Thee is hell,
 To walk with Thee is heaven.

> We faintly hear, we dimly see,
>   In differing phrase we pray;
> But, dim or clear, we own in Thee
>   The Light, the Truth, the Way.

ANOTHER HYMN BY JOHN GREENLEAF WHITTIER:
Dear Lord and Father of Mankind.

TUNES: *Bishopthorpe.*
       St. Hugh.

SOME hymns move us to tears (like " There is a Green Hill ");
some scatter our fears (like " Who Would True Valour See ");
others bring deep peace and calm. The hymns of John Greenleaf
Whittier are in this last class, though it must be pointed out
at once that his hymns were not written as such, but they have
been extracted from his longer poems. This is a very unusual
thing and it should be noted; there are very few similar cases.

But there is no doubt this hymn and others like " Dear Lord
and Father of Mankind " breathe an atmosphere which is bound
to bring peace to troubled hearts. What a ministry there is along
this line. Who has not been blessed and quietened by the
verse which runs like this?

> O Sabbath rest by Galilee!
>   O calm of hills above,
> Where Jesus knelt to share with Thee,
> The silence of eternity
>   Interpreted by Love.

There are some other lines of which I am' very fond. I
believe these were written by Whittier in a friend's autograph
book. It is just a couplet:

> " I know not the way I'm going
>   But well do I know my Guide."

It is very interesting at this point to recall that Whittier's
poems were often in the hands of David Livingstone. He found
them so helpful because of the rest which they conveyed. One
wonders whether Livingstone knew the couplet just quoted.

Among the manuscripts which he left there is one paragraph
which will interest all hymn lovers. In it he disclaims any
talent as a hymn writer and speaks most modestly of his work.
He says: " I am really not a hymn writer, for the good reason
that I know nothing of music. Only a very few of my pieces
were written for singing. A good hymn is the best use to

which poetry can be devoted, but I do not claim that I have succeeded in composing one."   Dr. Julian's estimate would appear to contradict this, for he asserts that his hymns are characterized by " rich, poetic beauty, sweet tenderness, a deep sympathy with human kind."   About 30 of his hymns are in common use.

His love of nature which comes out in all his work was born in him and fostered by his early life in the country. He was the son of a farmer in Massachusetts, where he had few chances of getting books to read. But a friendly schoolmaster lent him a copy of the poems of Robert Burns, which fired his genius and set him to work.

> How oft that day, with fond delay,
>   I sought the maple's shadow;
> And sang with Burns the hours away,
>   Forgetful of the meadow.

He was encouraged by his elder sister to publish some of his early verses which he sent to a newspaper edited by Wm. Lloyd Garrison, the great journalist abolitionist. The editor was so impressed by these poems that he rode out the 75 miles to Whittier's home to meet his new contributor, and so began a long and loyal friendship. Garrison and Whittier fought the slave trade together, and no one will know how much Whittier's poems contributed to its eventual abolition. In my copy of his poems there are over 100 pages devoted to this subject, and this is only part of his work along this line. His stanzas to William Lloyd Garrison are unforgettable:

> Then onward with a martyr's zeal;
>   And wait thy rare reward
> When man to man no more shall kneel,
>   And God alone be Lord!

The poet's fame could well rest on one piece, " My Psalm," whose spiritual and mystic beauty has rarely been surpassed. I will not quote even one verse for fear I spoil your enjoyment of it. But after reading it again we can well understand how Whittier has been called " America's greatest lyrical and most distinctively religious poet."

For about 20 years in middle life he was a most successful journalist and editor, poems flowing all the way along from his ready pen. Ten or eleven years of his life were taken up with busy activity as Secretary of the American-Anti-Slavery Society. After retirement he removed to Amesbury, a village in Massachusetts, not far from his birthplace.

All through his life he was a Quaker, wearing to the end the peculiar garb of the early Friends and always using their quaint forms of speech. He was very fond of the second person singular! His Quaker background and convictions must not be forgotten when using his hymns and reading his poetry. He has sometimes been accused of unitarian leanings but we notice again and again his adoration of Christ his Divine Master. In the poem from which this hymn is taken occur the lines:

> Strike deep Thy roots, O heavenly vine,
>   Within our earthly sod.
> Most human and yet most divine,
>   The flower of man and God.

The hymn before us is taken from a long poem entitled " Our Master " (1866), written after the Civil War was over and slavery abolished. It reflects all through the poet's sense of God's near presence and His unfailing Providence. If possible the hymn should be read in this larger context. I will not comment on the six verses which are usually sung, but pick out my favourite verse:

> But warm, sweet, tender, even yet
>   A present help is He:
> And faith has still its Olivet,
>   And love its Galilee.

What a theme for meditation these three ephithets present to us! Let us all ponder the warmth, the sweetness, the tenderness, of the Lord Jesus Christ. These words might have been written by Faber. A word of the Psalmist comes to mind, " Thy gentleness hath made me great " (Psalm 18: 35).

I cannot close this article without giving what to me is his most priceless and perfect gem. Here it is:

> "I know not where His islands lift
>   Their fronded palms in air;
> I only know, I cannot drift
>   Beyond His love and care."

I heard the voice of Jesus say

HORATIUS BONAR
1808-1889

I heard the voice of Jesus say,
  " Come unto Me and rest;
Lay down, thou weary one, lay down
  Thy head upon My breast."
I came to Jesus as I was,
  Weary and worn and sad,
I found in Him a resting-place,
  And He has made me glad.

I heard the voice of Jesus say,
  " Behold I freely give
The living water; thirsty one,
  Stoop down, and drink, and live."
I came to Jesus, and I drank
  Of that life-giving stream,
My thirst was quench'd, my soul revived,
  And now I live in Him.

I heard the voice of Jesus say,
  " I am this dark world's light,
Look unto Me, thy morn shall rise,
  And all thy day be bright."
I look'd to Jesus, and I found
  In Him my Star, my Sun;
And in that light of life I'll walk,
  Till travelling days are done.

OTHER HYMNS BY HORATIUS BONAR:

Here, O My Lord, I See Thee Face to Face.
Thy Way, Not Mine, O Lord.
I Hear the Words of Love.

TUNES : *Vox Dilecti.*
          Kingsfold.

ONE evening in a south coast seaside town this lovely hymn was being sung at the close of an open-air service. Many were standing round listening, others passed slowly by and only caught a word or a line of the hymn. One who walked casually by was captivated by one line — a line which gave the answer to the spiritual darkness within his soul. The line was

" I am this dark world's light." The hearing of that line borne home to the burdened conscience by the Holy Spirit meant that yet another soul passed from darkness into Christ's most marvellous light.

One is quite confident that this is one instance of hundreds which will be revealed in the great day when the secrets of all hearts will be revealed, for this hymn is a great favourite at Mission services. It never fails to make a special appeal and I have found that it is a great favourite with children, perhaps on account of its simplicity. The personal note which is so prominent in the hymn is very penetrating, and it is not the kind of hymn one can sing without making an individual response. We know unmistakeably that the hymn either records our history or it does not; there is no middle ground.

The great Bishop James Fraser of Manchester described this hymn as the best in the English language. Bishop Handley Moule in a memorial volume on Horatius Bonar says that all his hymns have a rare power of moving the conscience, and he gives as the reason that they are full of Scripture. I would say that two elements are always prominent — a clear vision of Christ as Saviour and frequent reference to the Second Advent.

The four hymns included in " Hymns Ancient and Modern " are very well known: " The Church Has Waited Long," " I Was a Wandering Sheep," " A Few More Years Shall Roll," " I Heard the Voice of Jesus Say." But there are others which are very precious: " Thy Way, Not Mine, O Lord," " Here, O My Lord, I See Thee Face to Face."

Not long after his death an article appeared in the *Sunday Magazine* for March, 1897, by his daughter, in which the view was emphasized that his poetry is largely autobiographical. A lady in England wrote to the writer of the article to thank her and added that the hymns of Dr. Bonar had " nerved her when she was lagging in the race, cheered her in sorrow and trial, and kept her watching for the coming of the Lord."

" There is nobody like Bonar for singing about Heaven," exclaims one of the characters in Mrs. Ward's " Gates Ajar." The hymns of Bonar and Bernard of Cluny are very much alike. " Is Bonar the hymn writer still alive?" was the question of a stranger to a member of his congregation. " I always thought he was a medieval saint." But Bonar had an assurance and a joy of which most medieval saints knew very little. There is however, an " other worldliness " about his hymns which some might associate with the cloister, but the heavenly-mindedness is in order to make us more holy and more fruitful on earth.

Duffield in his " English Hymns " says of Bonar's two little devotional books, " God's Way of Peace " and " God's Way of Holiness " that " they would relieve many a troubled Christian if he would turn to them in preference to abstract theology." The former has been much used by God. I know a man who as a High Church Curate was led to Christ through reading it. It was a great favourite with Canon Christopher, who for 50 years was Rector of St. Aldate's, Oxford. He gave it away to many undergraduates, advising them to begin with chapter 3 — " God's Character — Our Resting Place."

The story of his life is quickly told, though it was a distinguished and a long one. Leith, Kelso and Edinburgh were the three scenes of his ministry, after a notable career at Edinburgh High School and University. He was a pupil of Thomas Chalmers at the University, and followed his old teacher in seceding from the Church of Scotland in 1843 and forming the Free Church. Bonar was one of the 474 ministers who went forth at the time of the disruption " not knowing whither but knowing full well with whom." It must have been a great sacrifice to turn their backs upon Churches and congregations and stipends and homes for conscience sake. Bonar was made Moderator of the General Assembly in 1883, which is the highest honour the Church can confer.

I love what one of Bonar's sons said of his father after his death. " So skilfully did he exercise guidance as a father that I never felt the rein that was driving me. I admired his strength and firmness and as a schoolboy I felt him to be always fair. He laid himself out to be approachable and he continually invited my confidence. He liked me to tell him everything and he was easy to come to." It should not be forgotten that Horatius had an equally distinguished brother, Andrew, whose nickname was " Sunny Andrew." His line was more devotional writing than hymns.

Turning our attention now to the three well known verses of this hymn, we notice first its general character. Each of the three verses is divided into a call from the Lord and our corresponding response, " I came . . . I drank . . . I looked." And how many have heard His voice and He ours as this hymn has been sung. Charlotte Elliott's " Just as I am " is in the same class and both have been widely used at evangelistic services.

(1) *Our restlessness and His rest.* The oft-quoted words at the end of Matt. 11 — words of which we never tire — form the Saviour's call: Christ *is* the rest He offers; it is not a blessing apart from the Blesser, but a combination of both. I find a resting place in Him. Rest . . . a resting place. The heart is restless, said Augustine at the beginning of his Confessions, until it rests in Christ. And with the rest comes gladness, joy unspeakable, full of glory.

(2) *Our thirst and His supply.* Connect up two verses, one in the Gospel, the other in the Apocalypse. " If any man thirst, let him come unto Me and drink " (John 7: 37). " And whosoever will, let him take the water of life freely " (Rev. 22: 17). It is said that a thirsty traveller in the desert will part with any and all of his possessions to get water. Water! Water! Water! He must have it. I came to Jesus and I drank . . . my thirst was quenched. He satisfies the longing soul but we must be ready to stoop down. The water of Life is for the lowly.

(3) *Our darkness and His Light.* That wanderer by the sea heard the call. " I am this dark world's light . . . Look unto me," and the answer, " I looked." We think of Saul of Tarsus who saw Christ clad in a glory above the brightness of the sun, and he looked and in the light of Life he travelled right on to the end of the road, and the Light never failed. And His promise holds good, " But the path of the righteous is as the light of dawn that shineth more and more unto the perfect day " (Prov. 4: 18, marg.)

Come, ye thankful people, come

HENRY ALFORD
1810-1871

Come, ye thankful people, come,
 Raise the song of Harvest-home:
All is safely gather'd in,
 Ere the winter storms begin:
God, our Maker, doth provide
 For our wants to be supplied.
Come to God's own temple, come,
 Raise the song of Harvest-home.

All the world is God's own field,
    Fruit unto His praise to yield;
Wheat and tares together sown,
    Unto joy or sorrow grown:
First the blade, and then the ear,
    Then the full corn shall appear:
Lord of harvest, grant that we
    Wholesome grain and pure may be.

For the Lord our God shall come,
    And shall take His harvest home:
From His field shall in that day
    All offences purge away;
Give His angels charge at last
    In the fire the tares to cast,
But the fruitful ears to store
    In His garner evermore.

Even so, Lord, quickly come
    To Thy final Harvest-home:
Gather Thou Thy people in,
    Free from sorrow, free from sin;
There for ever purified,
    In Thy presence to abide:
Come, with all Thine angels, come,
    Raise the glorious Harvest-home.

OTHER HYMNS BY HENRY ALFORD:

Forward Be Our Watchword.
Ten Thousand Times Ten Thousand.

TUNE: *St. George* (Elvey).

I KNOW a gentleman who if the Harvest Festival service does not begin with this hymn feels like walking out, even if he does not do so! I suppose there must be many like that. Like several other hymns, for instance Kipling's " Recessional " or Baring Gould's " Onward Christian Soldiers," this hymn was written for a special occasion, a service of thanksgiving for harvest. Several of his hymns were called forth in this way, notably, " Forward Be Our Watchword."

He was born in London in 1810 and in 1829 entered Trinity College, Cambridge, for which he had been coached by his father, who was a scholarly clergyman. He was thrown very much with his father because his mother died when he was born, and he often acknowledged his debt to his father who led him to faith in Christ and then nourished that faith. Incumbent of Wymeswold, Leicester (1835-53) and then Quebec Chapel, in 1857 he became Dean of Canterbury, a position which he held for fourteen years until his death in 1871.

During his life he was known as one of the most versatile clergymen alive — poet, preacher, painter, musician, critic, traveller and Biblical scholar. He was one of those responsible for the Revised Version of the Bible. He wrote a commentary on the Greek Testament which is still very valuable; it was the fruit of twenty years work. He had a deeply reverent attitude to Scripture and his Preface to the Commentary is most striking. It is interesting to note that after a long day's work he contrived to " Stand up as at the end of a meal and thank God for what he had received."

He married his cousin, Fanny Alford, and they read the New Testament in the original together. Her biography of him contains a good many of their letters, which are very remarkable. In one of them during their engagement he wrote: " I entreat and conjure you by everything you value if you have any regard for my temporal and spiritual welfare, to do your utmost to cure me of that sharpness and spirit of opposition which so often shews itself in me."

They had many sorrows in their home life, and one of Alford's hymns, " Ten Thousand Times Ten Thousand," was called forth by bereavement. " Our thoughts have been much turned of late to the eternal state. Half our children are there and where the treasure is, there will the heart be also."

A pathetic entry was made in his *Journal*, 17th July, 1866: " Sixteen years since our boy Ambrose died. What would he have been now? Yes, but what *is* he now?" On his own grave is the inscription written by himself, " *Deversorum Viatoris Hierosolymam Proaciscentis* " — the inn of a traveller on his way to Jerusalem.

Let me tell you a story about him before we consider the hymn in detail. In 1854 Lord Chancellor Cranworth offered Dean Alford a post in Lincs. The Dean, who had made up his mind to decline it, went to the Chancellor's house to thank him. When he asked to see him the servant said his master was engaged. " But tell him," said the Dean, " that it is not a person who has come to ask for anything, but one who wishes to refuse something that has been offered." " Oh, sir!"

D

was the answer, " in that case I am sure he will see you!"

VERSE 1. Bishop Walsham How used to assert that this hymn is one of the most jubilant in the book, and this verse by itself substantiates that claim. " Thou shalt keep the feast of harvest " (Exodus 23: 15-16), God has said, and one feels that it is a perpetual command. Harvest is a time of great joy when we realise the fulfilment of God's promise to supply our needs and it is this thought which is emphasized in the first verse. We gather in God's temple to raise the song of harvest home and to thank Him for " His smile upon man's industry." " Come " is one of God's favourite words; it grieves Him to say " depart."

VERSE 2. From the idea of the material harvest we pass to the spiritual, and this verse recalls Christ's words in Matthew 13 and Mark 4. Through the sowing of the seed of Eternal Life in the heart, by the Holy Spirit, we become wholesome and pure grain for His garner. The seed is the Word of God and when it is sown it must not be choked by thorns and snatched away by the fowls of the air. And let us not forget that the tares which grow with the wheat are very much like the wheat. The enemy sows the tares and one can soon test whether one is a tare or not; " Have I renounced the Devil and all his works?"

VERSE 3. Next we come to a searching verse about the last day, Christ's Harvest Home, His return in glory. How sad the cry of those who must say, " The harvest is past, the summer is ended, and we are not saved." " Gather ye together first the tares, and bind them in bundles to burn them." This verse always makes me marvel that the hymn is so popular. Is it that the meaning of the words do not sink in? Perhaps the fact that it is only sung once a year has something to do with it.

VERSE 4. The two alternatives are again before us " In the fire . . . In Thy presence," but the emphasis is upon the latter. In His Presence we are to be " free from sorrow, free from sin," " purified," and all this for ever because there we are to " abide." Our minds quickly pass to the passages at the end of the Revelation where those scenes and experiences at the end are so perfectly described. There we find the last promise: " Truly, I come quickly," and the last prayer, " Even so, come, Lord Jesus," and the last provision, " The grace of the Lord Jesus Christ be with you all. Amen."

Fight the good fight with all thy might

JOHN SAMUEL BEWLEY MONSELL
1811-1875

Fight the good fight with all thy might,
 Christ is thy strength, and Christ thy right;
Lay hold on life, and it shall be
 Thy joy and crown eternally.

Run the straight race through God's good grace,
 Lift up thine eyes, and seek His face;
Life with its way before us lies,
 Christ is the path, and Christ the prize.

Cast care aside, lean on thy Guide;
 His boundless mercy will provide;
Lean, and the trusting soul shall prove,
 Christ is its life, and Christ its love.

Faint not, nor fear, His arms are near,
 He changeth not, and thou art dear;
Only believe, and thou shalt see
 That Christ is all in all to thee.

OTHER HYMNS BY J. S. B. MONSELL:

I Hunger and I Thirst.
O Worship the Lord in the Beauty of Holiness.

TUNES: *Pentecost.*
    Duke Street.

THE thought of the Christian life as warfare is very prominent in St. Paul's Epistles, and the idea has been taken up in a good many hymns. " Fight the good fight of faith, lay hold on eternal life " (1 Tim. 6: 12). This is a striking passage on which no doubt the hymn is based, but there are others. We remember the " armour " passage in Eph. 6 and the " training " passage in Psalm 144. But of course the hymn is not all about spiritual conflict; as we shall see, other activities come into view.

Remembering this it causes surprise that the hymn should have been such a favourite in the South African War and also the war waged by the United States over the Philippine Islands in 1898. Doubtless it is because of the " strenuous " note throughout, as well as the martial allusion in the first verse. It is a great favourite with boys, and the Boys' Brigade tell us it is asked for more than any other. Its straightforwardness and its challenge are sufficient explanation for popularity in these quarters. It is interesting to recall that it first appeared in Ferguson's Selection of Hymns for British Seamen, 1838, and was headed " Valiant for the Truth."

Dr. Monsell died as a result of an accident at the age of 64, on 9th August, 1875. Entering his Church at Guildford, which was being restored, a mass of stonework fell on him and cut his head very badly, as he was observing the progress being made. As a result of the blow he was knocked unconscious, and from this condition he never recovered. It was an unexpected ending to a good man's life, but as with George Whitefield " Sudden death was sudden glory."

He was born in Londonderry 2nd March, 1811, in that old town of so many stirring memories. He went to St. Columb's School in the town, from which he passed to Trinity College, Dublin, the *alma mater* of so many famous Irishmen. Ordained in 1834, he became successively Chaplain to Bishop Mant, Chancellor of the Diocese of Connor, and Rector of Ramoan. He resigned the latter benefice on his appointment to the Vicarage of Egham, Worcester, whence he moved to Guildford, to the parish of St. Nicholas, in which he died at the height of his powers.

He was a very considerable poet, and those who are familiar with his devotional poems will know how stimulating they are. His *Parish Hymnal* after the order of the Book of Common Prayer (1873) is well worth consulting. Compilers of modern hymn books could certainly do worse than consult the poetical works of Dr. Monsell. If you consult his *Nursery Carols* you will make some pleasing discoveries. It is disappointing that so much of the fine work of this worthy Irishman has been lost in oblivion.

Julian enumerates 72 hymns and addresses: " Dr. Monsell's hymns are as a whole bright, joyous and musical, but they lack massiveness, concentration of thought and strong emotion. A few only are of enduring excellence." If one may venture to break a lance with the authority to whom every student of hymns is in the deepest debt, one may suggest that the hymn before us is as massive as any of equal compass.

Dr. Monsell's views on hymns were that "they should be more fervent and joyous. We are too distant and reserved in our praises. We sing not as we should sing to Him and of Him who is chief among 10,000, the altogether lovely."

His hymns issued from a very happy home. One who knew it well writes: "It was quite an ideal household, full of the beauty of holiness, with genial brightness and gaiety playing like sunshine over all the troubles of life." Of such a home we can say, "Christ is its Life and Christ its Love."

There is something pathetic about his last poem, which was written to raise funds for the rebuilding of the Church. The first four lines proved to be a prophecy.

> Dear Body, thou and I must part,
> Thy busy head, thy throbbing heart,
> Must cease to work, must cease to play,
> For me at no far distant day.

A few weeks afterwards they did part, until the resurrection morning. One can imagine what heart-searching was in the Guildford parish for some time after their beloved pastor had gone.

Four characters are before us in these four verses of this stimulating hymn, which is Pauline in its strength. Monsell uses figures of which the Apostle was very fond. We see the Soldier, the Athlete, the Pilgrim, the Believer.

(1) *The Soldier.* The parodox of the Christian fight is that we are to fight with all our might and yet we are to renounce our strength for Christ is our strength. Our strength is as the strength of ten not just because our hearts are pure, but because He who is our strength dwells within. "I can do all things in Christ who strengthens me."

(2) *The Athlete.* In 2 Tim. 2 St. Paul passes straight from the Army to the Athlete (3-5) as Monsell does. Maybe the translation of the hymn writer has this scriptural basis though we cannot be sure. Good it is to remember as we saw in verse 1, that grace for the race is furnished. His face is the goal, the inspiration of which is infinite and yet His face is not afar off but near, for Christ is the path. "I press towards the mark," Paul says in the Philippian letter.

(3) *The Pilgrim.* For every Pilgrim there is a Guide and an infallible one. He never misleads, but He must be consulted and we must keep near Him, without running before or lagging

behind. This Guide has what no human guide possesses, "boundless mercy and boundless power." "Guide me, O Thou great Jehovah, Pilgrim through this barren land."

(4) *The Believer.* The three foregoing characters are all concentrated and summed up in the last, the believer. "Only believe." "His arms are near." His will unchangeable, His heart most loving. "If thou wouldest believe, thou shouldest see the glory of God" (John 11: 40). The order is the spiritual biblical order; Come and see. "Seeing is believing," they tell us. But in this realm it is the other way about. "Lord, I believe, help Thou mine unbelief."

O Jesus, King most wonderful

EDWARD CASWALL
1814-1878

O Jesu, King most wonderful,
    Thou Conqueror renown'd,
Thou Sweetness most ineffable,
    In Whom all joys are found!

When once Thou visitest the heart,
    Then truth begins to shine,
Then earthly vanities depart,
    Then kindles love Divine.

O Jesu, Light of all below,
    Thou Fount of living fire,
Surpassing all the joys we know,
    And all we can desire:

Jesu, may all confess Thy Name,
    Thy wondrous love adore,
And, seeking Thee, themselves inflame
    To seek Thee more and more.

Thee, Jesu, may our voices bless,
    Thee may we love alone,
And ever in our lives express
    The image of Thine Own.

OTHER HYMNS BY EDWARD CASWALL:

See Amid the Winter Snow.
Days and Moments Quickly Flying.

TUNES: St. Agnes.
         Metzler's Redhead.
         Abridge.

MANY of our best hymns are translations from hymns in other languages. There are not many who had the skill to make such translations perfectly, but there have been cases where it has been thought that the translation is better than the original. Writers have made this claim for Edward Caswall and the hymn before us is a case in point.

Like Ray Palmer's " Jesus Thou Joy of Loving Hearts," this hymn has its source in a celebrated Latin poem written by Bernard of Clairvaux, the Cistercian monk who lived in the twelfth century. The poem was circulated in 1140 and entitled " Jesus dulci memoria." It glows all the way through with a deep love for the Redeemer which Bernard experienced more and more as he engaged in controversy with Peter Abelard.

Bernard's poem was a favourite with David Livingstone and it often comforted and strengthened him as he trudged through the wilds of Africa. " That hymn of St. Bernard, in the name of Christ; although in what might be termed dog-Latin, pleases me so; it rings in my ears as I wander across the wild, wild wilderness. When one writes a hymn on the name of Christ one never knows where its inspiration will go, and of Bernard it may truly be said, " He being dead yet speaketh." Is it any wonder that Luther spoke of Bernard as " The best monk that ever lived."

Edward Caswall has some lovely hymns: " See Amid the Winter Snow," " When Morning Gilds the Skies," " Days and Moments Quickly Flying," but none so beautiful and so touching as this one — " O Jesus, King Most Wonderful." No hymn forms a better expression of the rapture of the new convert and it is because we are converts to the end of our days that we love it so much.

Let me tell you something of the life and work of Edward Caswall. The son of a clergyman, he was born at Yately, Hants., of which his father was Vicar, on 15th July, 1814. He took an honours degree from Brasenose College, Oxford, and was ordained in 1838. While at the University he wrote a satire on the idle and wasteful habits of his fellow undergraduates called " The Art of Pluck," which is still referred to. After a short curacy he was preferred to the Vicarage of Stratford-cum-Castle near Salisbury in 1840, and remained there seven years.

In 1847 he resigned his position and with his wife entered

the Church of Rome. After his wife died in 1850 from cholera, he was ordained priest in the Roman Communion and joined Newman at Birmingham. He helped Newman to establish the Oratory at Edgbaston. For nearly 30 years they lived together, but Caswall was not drawn into public controversy. He continued his translation, his clerical duties, and his work among the poor, of which he was very fond. Newman wrote of him, " He was a very humble man — every good deed others did was wonderful to him; what he himself did was nothing."

As a translator Julian ranks him next to J. M. Neale, and a contemplation of this hymn confirms such a view. One might almost put Caswall first and above Neale. While being strictly faithful to his originals, Caswall excells in the purity of his rhythm, which makes his hymns perfect poetry and very easy to sing. They are ideal for congregational use. It is a great tribute to his ability as a translator that very few of his original compositions are in common use. His forte was in translation and we are grateful for his fine work in this direction.

One hundred and ninety-seven translations appeared in Lyra Catholica, 1849. These were from the Roman Breviary Missal and other sources. In 1873 most of these reappeared in a volume entitled, " Hymns and Poems," together with other pieces.

The hymn before us is a eulogy of our Lord Jesus Christ as the source of all blessing. It lifts up the name of the Saviour high above all. Its simplicity is such that it appeals very much to children, and yet it is comprehensive. It forms a precious commentary on the Song of Solomon where the Bridegroom is so glowingly extolled. As one reads through the hymn there are no special passages which come to mind as probably in the mind of the writer: rather is it a question of the verses being parallel to some of Christ's titles and expressing our delight as we contemplate this.

(1) Connect Verse 1 with Isaiah 9: 6:

" For unto us a Child is born, unto us a Son is given; and the government shall be upon His shoulder: and His name shall be called Wonderful, Counsellor, the mighty God, the everlasting Father, The Prince of Peace."

(2) Connect Verse 2 with Isaiah 26: 13:

" O Lord our God, other lords beside Thee have had dominion over us: but by Thee only will we make mention of Thy name."

(3) Connect Verse 3 with the Song of Solomon, 5: 16:

" He is altogether lovely " — Himself the concentration of loveliness (lit.).

(4) Connect Verse 4 with Hosea 6: 3:

" Then shall we know, if we follow on to know the Lord; His going forth is prepared as the morning; and He shall come unto us as the rain, as the latter and former rain unto the earth."

(5) Connect Verse 5 with 2 Cor. 3: 18:

" But we all, with open face, beholding as in a glass the glory of the Lord, are changed into the same image from glory to glory, even as by the Spirit of the Lord."

" I will extol thee, my God, O King; and I will bless Thy name for ever and ever." (Psa. 145: 1).

O Jesus, I have promised

JOHN ERNEST BODE
1816-1874

O Jesus, I have promised
  To serve Thee to the end;
Be Thou for ever near me,
  My Master and my Friend;
I shall not fear the battle
  If Thou art by my side,
Nor wander from the pathway
  If Thou wilt be my Guide.

Oh let me feel Thee near me:
  The world is ever near;
I see the sights that dazzle,
  The tempting sounds I hear;
My foes are ever near me,
  Around me and within;
But, Jesus, draw Thou nearer,
  And shield my soul from sin.

Oh let me hear Thee speaking
  In accents clear and still,
Above the storms of passion,
  The murmurs of self-will;
Oh speak to re-assure me,
  To hasten, or control;
Oh speak, and make me listen,
  Thou Guardian of my soul.

O Jesus, Thou hast promised
　　To all who follow Thee,
That where Thou art in glory
　　There shall Thy servant be;
And, Jesus, I have promised
　　To serve Thee to the end,
Oh give me grace to follow,
　　My Master and my Friend.

O let me see Thy footmarks
　　And in them plant mine own
My hope to follow duly
　　Is in Thy strength alone.
Oh guide me, call me, draw me,
　　Uphold me to the end;
And then in heaven receive me,
　　My Saviour and my Friend.

OTHER HYMNS BY J. E. BODE:

God of Heaven, Enthroned in Might.
Spirit of Truth, Indwelling Light.

TUNES:　*Day of Rest.*
　　　　　Wolvercote.

SOME hymn writers are known by just one hymn. They may
have written others, but one has gained prominence and
permanence and will never die. This is a comparatively rare
thing, for most hymn writers have given us a number of hymns,
but occasionally it is just one that has been singled out. This
is the case with the hymn we are considering. John Bode wrote
a good many hymns, but the average man could not mention a
companion to " O Jesus I Have Promised." He did in fact
write a series of hymns based on the Gospels for the Sundays
of the year and the festivals of the year, something like Keble's
" Christian Year," but the collection has been largely forgotten.
This hymn was written by John Bode for the occasion when
three of his children, two sons and a daughter, were to be confirmed at Castle Camps, Cambridge. The hymn was to impress
upon their minds the solemnity of the step they were taking
that day. And ever since it has been associated with confirm-
ations and first communions. Few confirmation services are
held without it being sung, and it certainly does make a fine
climax, especially when sung to the tune " Day of Rest," with

which the hymn is usually associated. But when the hymn is sung at other times it always awakens memories of the vows previously made.

John Ernest Bode, the son of Mr. Wm. Bode of the G.P.O., was born in 1816, and educated at Eton and Christchurch, Oxford. In due course he was ordained and became Rector of Westwell, Oxon, in 1846; and then of Castle Camps, Cambridge, in 1860, where he remained until his death. He was also for a time Tutor at Christ Church and Classical Examiner. It appears that he lived an uneventful though exemplary life as a country clergyman, fulfilling his ministry in a quiet sphere.

He was Bampton Lecturer in 1855 on the foundation of John Bampton at Oxford. And in addition to the poems already mentioned he published " Short Occasional Poems " in 1858. In the most part these were mainly of passing interest.

The hymn we are looking at first appeared in the form of a leaflet (No. 1468) issued by the Society for Promoting Christian Knowledge in 1868 — as a hymn for the newly confirmed. It had then six verses instead of the five usually sung, and I must give the sixth in a moment.

The next year, 1869, it was included in the Appendix to S.P.C.K. Psalms and Hymns. Later on it appeared in Hymns Ancient and Modern.

The missing verse goes like this: —

> " Oh! let me see thy features
>   The look that once could make
> So many a true disciple
>   Leave all things for Thy sake.
> The look that beamed on Peter
>   When he Thy name denied;
> The look that draws Thy lovers
>   Close to Thy piercèd side."

No one but God knows the many vows and promises which have been made to Christ during the singing of this hymn, but when the secrets of all hearts shall be revealed it will make a wonderful story. How glad the author will be. Doubtless he thought his hymn was just for the benefit of his family, but he wrote better than he knew. Let me pick out three prayers in the hymn from the verses usually sung, omitting the similar prayer in the verse which is often omitted:

(1) *O! Let me feel Thee near me*: This is a prayer for Christ's presence, especially for a realization of it. Where two or three are gathered in His name He is in the midst, but even so we do not always recollect His presence. We do not need to ask Him to come, but we must ask that He will make His presence *felt*. Oh! Let me *feel* Thee near me. Jesus Himself drew near and went with them — this is our desire. The disciples knew not that it was Jesus (John 21: 4), but it was, and they needed to *feel* His presence. "He is come, Austen, He is come," said a dying martyr to his friend, as he felt Christ's presence.

(2) *Oh! Let me hear Thee speaking.* So many other voices claim our attention. There is so much speaking today, and not least powerful is the voice of self within. We need to *hear* Christ speaking. "Speak, Lord, for Thy servant heareth" must be our prayer. The voice of the Lord bringeth mighty things to pass (see Psalm 29). "And His that gentle voice we hear ... that checks each thought." He heard the voice of Jesus say "Come unto Me, and rest." "I heard behind me a great voice." "Thine ears shall hear a word behind thee, saying, 'This is the way.'"

(3) *Oh! Let me see Thy footmarks.* How grand it is that the Lord has promised to go before us. It is not an untried way. "I will go before thee and make the rough places plain." Recall the words of Bunyan in *Pilgrim's Progress*: "I have loved to hear my Lord spoken of and wherever I have seen the print of His shoe in the earth, there have I coveted to set my foot also."

Let me close this study with the words of David Livingstone, for the hymn ends not on our promise, but Christ's "O, Jesus, *Thou* hast promised." The great missionary was in danger in Central Africa, and he wrote in his diary, "Felt much turmoil of spirit in view of having all my plans knocked on the head by savages tomorrow. But Jesus said, 'I am with you always, even unto the end of the world.' It is the word of a Gentleman of the strictest honour, and there's an end on't. I will not cross secretly by night, as I intended. It would appear as flight. I shall take observations for latitude and longitude this evening, though they may be the last. I feel quite calm now, thank God."

Jerusalem the Golden

JOHN MASON NEALE
1818-1866

Jerusalem the golden,
    With milk and honey bless'd,
Beneath thy contemplation
    Sink heart and voice oppress'd;
I know not, O, I know not,
    What joys await us there;
What radiancy of glory,
    What bliss beyond compare.

They stand, those halls of Zion,
    All jubilant with song,
And bright with many an angel,
    And all the martyr throng;
The Prince is ever in them,
    The daylight is serene;
The pastures of the blessed
    Are deck'd in glorious sheen.

There is the throne of David;
    And there from care released,
The shout of them that triumph,
    The song of them that feast;
And they who with their Leader
    Have conquer'd in the fight,
For ever and for ever
    Are clad in robes of white.

O sweet and blessed country,
    The Home of God's elect!
O sweet and blessed country,
    That eager hearts expect!
Jesu, in mercy bring us
    To that dear land of rest!
Who art, with God the Father,
    And Spirit, ever blest.

OTHER HYMNS BY J. M. NEALE:

O Come, O Come, Emmanuel.
O Happy Band of Pilgrims.

TUNE: *Ewing.*

JOHN MASON NEALE was born in 1818, the son of " pronounced evangelical parents." His father was a clergyman, the Rev. Cornelius Neale, who had a distinguished career at Cambridge and became Second Chancellor's Medallist as well as Senior Wrangler. His mother was the daughter of John Mason Good, a man of considerable learning, whose names were given to his grandson.

He was a most voluminous writer; hymns, sermons and letters coming from his pen in quick succession. It is amazing that he packed so much into so short a life. One might almost think that there was some mistake in the dates 1818-1866. He died when he was 48, worn out, it is likely, by his strenuous labours and the difficulties he had to face.

He was ordained in 1841, appointed Vicar of Crawley in 1843, where he married Miss Sarah Webster, the daughter of an evangelical clergyman. But the work of Crawley was too much for him and his health soon broke down, and he was obliged to go abroad. But doubtless this was part of God's plan, for it brought him into touch with continental hymns, and especially with the Eastern Church, of which he wrote a history.

In 1846 he was presented by Lord De la Warr to the Wardenship of Sackville College, East Grinstead, where he spent the rest of his short life. This appointment was worth £27 a year, and one wonders how he made ends meet. He rebuilt the college Chapel and founded an Orphanage and Sisterhood of East Grinstead. He died 6th July, 1866. On his coffin there was an inspiration he had written himself and it is full of pathos: —

" J. M. Neale, miser et indignus sacerdos requiescens sub Signo Thau. (J. M. Neale, poor and unworthy priest resting under the sign of the cross).

Patient, humorous and prodigiously learned, J. M. Neale was one of the most remarkable men of his time. He had a vivid sense of the unseen and supernatural, with the faith of a child, and one can see this coming out in his hymns. He was very fond of little children, for whom he wrote stories and little hymns. As a linguist he had few equals, being a master of twelve languages and acquainted with eight others.

One of his greatest gifts was a genius for translation. It has been said that his verses in English were better than the originals, and one can believe it, for they " flow " in a way which disguises the fact that they are translations. His facility in this direction may be illustrated by an anecdote which reveals his mastery of Latin. It took place at Hursley when he was visiting John Keble.

" Mr. Keble, having to go to another room to find some papers, was detained a short time. On his return, Dr. Neale said, " Why, Keble, I thought you told me that the *Christian Year* was entirely original?" " Yes," he answered, " it certainly is". " Then how comes this?" and Dr. Neale placed before him the Latin of one of Keble's hymns. Keble professed himself utterly confounded. He protested that he had never seen this " original ", no, not in all his life. After a few minutes Neale relieved him by owning that he had just turned it into Latin in his absence!"

Let me mention two other points which indicate the character of the man. He held the view very firmly that all hymns, whether original or translated, ought to become the property of Christendom as soon as published, the author retaining no private privilege in connection with them. He stated this in a preface to a collection of translations. The idea of "copyright" was anathema to him. Over his study mantelpiece he had a motto which sums up his life, " Per angusta ad augusta " — " By the strait to the great."

There are some hymns which are wedded to a tune, and one never hears them sung to any other. The one printed above is in this category, the tune " Ewing " fitting it perfectly. Neale had several friends who set his hymns to music as he had no gift in this way, and as he said, " not a note in his voice."

These theme of the hymn is the heavenly Jerusalem to which we who believe have come (Heb. 12: 22). The feelings of the Jewish pilgrims going to Jerusalem, as we find them expressed in Psalm 84, are lifted up to a higher level, and we are transported to the " City of the Great King," which is described in the closing parts of the book of Revelation. " Jerusalem," " Zion," " The Throne of David," " Home," these terms taken from each of the four verses take us in thought to the city which was the joy of the whole earth.

We see Jerusalem and especially the temple, lit up by the glory of the setting sun, but the word " golden " reminds us of that city where the streets are pure gold, and we are overwhelmed by the wonder of that glorious place as we contemplate it.

In verse 2 we pass from the thought of the city to that of its inhabitants; the angels, the martyr throng, above all, the Prince Himself. What company! The last words of Hugh McHail in 1661 as he stood on the scaffold come to mind:

" Farewell, father and mother, friends and relations . . . Welcome God and Father; welcome sweet Jesus, the Mediator of the new covenant; welcome blessed Spirit of grace and God of all consolation; welcome glory; welcome eternal life . . . "

Verse three describes the occupants of the city and their employments. " They rest from their labours but they rest not day nor night " (Rev. 14: 13 and 4: 8) from their holy activities. Every care left behind, the last battle fought and won, they are clad in white, wearing the robes of victory.

The last verse is an apostrophe to that blessed country and a prayer that we may be brought safely there to that dear land of rest. The sweep and the simplicity of this glorious hymn reaches a climax as we address the blessed Trinity, Father, Son and Holy Spirit. And what a ring there is in the word " Home " — the home of God's elect. David Smith translates 2 Thess. 2: 1 as " Our gathering home unto Him."

We must leave this old favourite there, and as we do so let us be quite sure that with a vision of the next life we shall find inspiration for this.

What a friend we have in Jesus

JOSEPH SCRIVEN
1820-1886

What a Friend we have in Jesus
    All our sins and griefs to bear!
What a privilege to carry
    Everything to God in prayer!
O, what peace we often forfeit!
    O! what needless pain we bear!
All because we do not carry
    Everything to God in prayer.

Have we trials and temptations?
　　Is there trouble anywhere?
We should never be discouraged;
　　Take it to the Lord in prayer.
Can we find a friend so faithful
　　Who will all our sorrows share?
Jesus knows our every weakness;
　　Take it to the Lord in prayer.

Are we weak and heavy laden,
　　Cumbered with a load of care?
Precious Saviour, still our refuge —
　　Take it to the Lord in prayer.
Do thy friends despise, forsake thee?
　　Take it to the Lord in prayer;
In His arms He'll take and shield thee,
　　Thou wilt find a solace there.

TUNE:　*Converse.*

THE origin of our hymns is a very interesting line of enquiry, full of unexpected discoveries and joys. Hymns have been written for all sorts of purposes. Some like the hymns of Frances Alexander, were written specially for children to help them learn the Lord's Prayer, the Creed, and the Ten Commandments. Some, like George Matheson's touching masterpiece, were written to express the author's convictions and longings in connection with them. Some, like Baring Gould's "Onward Christian Soldiers," were written for a specific act of worship. Some, like Toplady's hymn included in this series of studies, arose out of some peculiar circumstance of life. Some arose spontaneously out of a devotional hour with the Saviour and were written down almost at His dictation.

The hymn now before us falls into the last category. It came to Joseph Scriven in his last illness as he thought of his mother whom he had to leave behind. We may say it arose from a Christian's desire to explain his own secret with a view to helping someone else who was very dear to him. Not long before Scriven was called Home, he was visited by a neighbour, who saw it written on a sheet of paper which lay on the table at his bedside. "Are you the author of this lovely poem?" asked the visitor. "The Lord and I did it together," was the reply. What a lovely explanation of the origin of this moving hymn, and maybe of most hymns. "The Lord and I did it together!" Do not these words let us into a great secret of

Christian living? What needless pain we bear because we try to do it on our own, and things go wrong, and we give way to self-pity. Do you remember what was said of Joseph in prison? Whatsoever they did there, He was the doer of it! Joseph is a type of his far greater descendant, the Lord Jesus Christ.

You may be surprised to know that this hymn arose out of a tragedy, though there was a long space of time between the actual tragedy and the completion of the hymn. There is not a great deal of information regarding Joseph Scriven, but such as we have I must give you, because I feel sure that this story will touch some readers very deeply, and may lead them in the path in which Scriven was led. It is a hymn for sufferers of all kinds, but specially for those who have had to face what Shakespeare calls " the slings of outrageous fortune," those in whose lives mysterious happenings have been permitted that it is hard to interpret.

Joseph Scriven was born in Ireland in 1820 and lived there for the first 25 years of his life. Some time in 1845 he emigrated to Canada as many another Irishman has done, seeking his fate in the New World. He died in 1886 at the age of 66, after a varied life filled with difficulties such as many a settler has known. He was brought to Christ as a result of losing his bride-to-be on the eve of their marriage. She was accidentally drowned a few hours before they were to be joined in holy matrimony. What an indescribable grief! How easily it might have led him in the opposite direction to unbelief and bitterness and hardness of heart. I always think of this when I come to the last lines of verse three:

> In His arms He'll take and shield thee;
> Thou wilt find a solace there.

It appears that the hymn was written a long time before it was seen by anyone save himself and his mother. It was written to comfort his mother in a time of great sorrow, and we can imagine what it meant to her after her son had died. How many hearts it has comforted since, no one knows but the Lord.

The subject of the hymn is the friendship of Christ, which is a very precious one, especially to the lonely and those in need. I remember an open air service in South London where this hymn was sung at the close. On the other side of the main road stood a young man who had just come to London to work, and he listened wistfully to all that was said and sung. The meeting over, he was approached by a worker, who asked him some questions in the strain, " Did you follow the address? etc., etc." But it seemed to mean nothing to the stranger until at last the young evangelist said, " Do you want a friend?" " Do I want a friend? I should think I do! I have just come up to London and don't know a soul!" And a friendship began that night which will never end.

Turning to the hymn itself, we note that there is a haunting refrain eight times repeated, " Take it to the Lord in prayer." " Everything to God in prayer " comes first; and then detail after detail for ever afterwards — take " it " to the Lord in prayer. We can summarize the three verses as follows: " our sins," " our sorrows," " our sighs." Are we facing " dispeace," " discomfort," " distress "? The same remedy suits every malady. The wording takes the form of question and answer, and every one who searches their heart with these interrogations will soon find the solution.

The note of intimate fellowship is seen throughout, fellowship between Christ and His friends. The Saviour carries our sins and knows our weaknesses and shields our hearts. Simplicity rather than profundity characterises this beautiful hymn which will ever be a favourite with women and children and all in need. Is there anything in the hymn which a child cannot understand? No words need explanation here! How easily this hymn might have been lost in oblivion if that precise piece of paper had been inadvertently destroyed.

May I suggest that these three verses are commentaries on three Scripture verses. Here are the passages, read them one by one, and then the verses of the hymn in between:

ISAIAH 48: 18: O that thou hadst hearkened to my commandments! then had thy peace been as a river. (Verse 1).

PROVERBS 18: 24: There is a friend that sticketh closer than a brother. (Verse 2).

MATTHEW 11: 28: Come unto Me, all ye that labour and are heavy laden, and I will give you rest. (Verse 3).

Thy hand, O God, has guided

EDWARD H. PLUMPTRE
1821-1891

Thy hand, O God, has guided
    Thy flock, from age to age;
The wondrous tale is written,
    Full clear, on every page;
Our fathers own'd Thy goodness,
    And we their deeds record;
And both of this bear witness,
    One Church, one Faith, one Lord.

Thy heralds brought glad tidings
    To greatest, as to least;
They bade men rise, and hasten
    To share the great King's feast;
And this was all their teaching,
    In every deed and word,
To all alike proclaiming
    One Church, one Faith, one Lord.

When shadows thick were falling,
    And all seem'd sunk in night,
Thou, Lord, didst send Thy servants,
    Thy chosen sons of light.
On them and on Thy people
    Thy plenteous Grace was pour'd,
And this was still their message,
    One Church, one Faith, one Lord.

Through many a day of darkness,
    Through many a scene of strife,
The faithful few fought bravely,
    To guard the Nation's life.
Their Gospel of redemption,
    Sin pardon'd, man restored,
Was all in this enfolded,
    One Church, one Faith, one Lord.

And we, shall we be faithless?
    Shall hearts fail, hands hang down?
Shall we evade the conflict,
    And cast away our crown?
Not so: in God's deep counsels
    Some better thing is stored;
We will maintain, unflinching,
    One Church, one Faith, one Lord.

Thy mercy will not fail us,
    Nor leave Thy work undone;
With Thy right hand to help us,
    The Victory shall be won;
And then, by men and angels,
    Thy Name shall be adored,
And this shall be their anthem,
    "One Church, one Faith, one Lord."

OTHER HYMNS BY E. H. PLUMPTRE:

Rejoice Ye Pure in Heart.
Thine Arm, O Lord, in Days of Old.

TUNES: *Thornbury.*
          Crüger.

THIS hymn is a stirring one which comes under the heading of "Church Defence." It is one of the most rousing hymns in any collection. If it is sung by a congregation of men it is not quickly forgotten. In some ways it is comparable to "Onward, Christian Soldiers." It draws inspiration from the past in order to stimulate effort in the present and to kindle inspiration for tasks that lie ahead.

The text which forms a title to this hymn is the verse from Ephesians, "There is one body and one spirit . . . one Lord, one faith, one baptism" (Eph. 4: 4-5). But an even better one could be chosen. "Upon this rock I will build My Church; and the gates of hell shall not prevail against it." That promise is a remarkable one. It suggests a militant Church which carries all before it, even the gates of hell being stormed and collapsing under its attacks. It must be confessed that usually the interpretation is the other way round and we are given a picture of the Church on the defensive reeling under the assaults of hell.

This is a great hymn, and something must be told about the great man from whose pen it came. It is almost impossible to exaggerate the learning, the culture and the industry of Dr. Plumptre. He had varied literary interests and excelled in them all. His greatest work was done as an expositor of the Bible, and I am going to call him the layman's expositor, and I'll tell you the reason later.

Edward Hayes Plumptre was educated at King's College, London, and University College, Oxford, graduating as a

Double First in 1844. Soon after his ordination in 1846 he made his mark as a preacher and was given rapid promotion. He became Professor of Pastoral Theology at King's College, London, Dean of Queen's College, Oxford, Professor of Exegesis of New Testament in King's College, London, in quick succession. His greatest distinction came when he was chosen as a member of the Old Testament Group for the Revision of the Authorised Version of the Holy Scriptures. In middle life we see him as Vicar of Bickley, in Kent, a position which he held for eight years, before being made Dean of Wells in 1881.

Besides his works of biblical exposition, he was distinguished as a translator of Æschylus and Dante. His own original verse should not be forgotten: Lazarus (1864), Master and Scholar (1866), Things New and Old (1884).

" As a writer of sacred poetry he ranks very high," is Julian's glowing tribute.

I called him just now " the layman's expositor." I did this because I have come across several outstanding laymen who are very fond of his writings, not least Dr. Eugene Stock, one of the great laymen of the last century, who was associated for so long with the C.M.S. Plumptre made a big contribution to Ellicott's Commentary published by Cassell's: Isaiah, Jeremiah, The Synoptic Gospels, Acts and 2 Corinthians; and anyone who works through these will be well repaid. Dr. Griffith Thomas characterizes the work as " illuminating and truly helpful."

Speaking generally of his poetry and hymns one cannot improve on what has been said by John Julian, " His hymns are elegant in style, fervent in spirit, and broad in treatment. The subjects chosen are mainly those associated with the revived Church life of the present day, from the Processional at a Choral Festival to hospital work and the spiritual life in schools and colleges. The rhythm of his verse has a special attraction for musicians, its poetry for the cultured, and its stately simplicity for the devout and earnest-minded."

Besides the one now under consideration, two others have been used extensively from the time of their composition. I mean the famous hospital hymn, " Thine Arm, O Lord, in Days of Old," and the hymn of joy which is almost an anthem, " Rejoice Ye Pure in Heart."

It is also interesting to recall that Plumptre wrote the

biography of another great hymn writer, Bishop Thomas Ken.

It is high time that we turned to the hymn itself, though it is too long to comment on each verse. The outstanding characteristic of the whole hymn is the closing line of each verse, " One Church, one Faith, one Lord " — which comes in with great power and effect even though the words are not exactly parallel to the Scripture, either in their order or content.

Let me try to recapitulate the theme which runs through the hymn:

God has unmistakeably guided our forefathers in the Church, having first sent His heralds to preach the Gospel and call men to share the feast. The only way to account for light coming into the darkness and scattering it is to say that God's plenteous grace was poured out, and even though at times God's army was few in number, He gave them the victory. The Gospel of redemption was preached and received. But what about ourselves? Shall we be faithless? No! it is impossible to fling away our crown and fail our great Captain, especially in view of the great future which lies before us. And also we have God's promise of unfailing help. His, the mercy, the work, the hand, the victory and the Name — so can we help being unflinching?

At the heart of the hymn there is a lovely line where God's grace overflows in the Gospel. It is this: " Sin pardoned, man restored." Is not this after all, the Church's best defence? Men who are forgiven for Christ's sake and re-created in God's image and after His likeness. In the singing of the last line, " One Church, one Faith, one *Lord*," the tune and the singing linger on the last word, LORD. There we will end as we began and as we will continue by God's grace.

There is a green hill far away

CECIL FRANCES ALEXANDER
1818-1895

There is a green hill far away,
    Without a city wall,
Where the dear Lord was crucified,
    Who died to save us all.

We may not know, we cannot tell,
    What pains He had to bear,
But we believe it was for us
    He hung and suffer'd there.

He died that we might be forgiven,
    He died to make us good,
That we might go at last to heaven,
    Saved by His precious blood.

There was no other good enough
    To pay the price of sin,
He only could unlock the gate
    Of heaven, and let us in.

Oh, dearly, dearly has He loved,
    And we must love Him too,
And trust in His redeeming blood,
    And try His works to do.

OTHER HYMNS BY MRS. C. F. ALEXANDER:

Once in Royal David's City.
All Things Bright and Beautiful.

TUNE: *Horsley.*

SOME of our best hymns were written by women. This is true of the one which is now to engage our attention. The three best-known authoresses are Frances Ridley Havergal, Fanny Crosby and Frances Alexander, all of whom were prolific hymn writers, and their work will last as long as hymns are sung.

Mrs. Alexander wrote many hymns which have become favourites, and it is difficult to know which one of hers to consider. We might, for instance, have taken " Once in Royal David's City," or " All things Bright and Beautiful." But we cannot err in choosing " There is a Green Hill Far Away." It is astonishing how popular this hymn is with boys; ask them to pick out a hymn they would like, and again and again this one will be suggested. Such a fact is a tribute in itself. Any hymn which has taken hold of a boy's mind and possessed it, is immortal.

Frances Alexander was an Irish lady, the wife of a country clergyman who afterwards became the Primate of all Ireland, the Archbishop of Armagh. Long before she was married, while still a girl, the poetic gift revealed itself and the poems she wrote were hidden under the carpet because she felt her parents would not approve of her devoting her time to such trivialities. But when her father discovered her poems, he read them carefully, encouraged her in her vocation, and decided to read them aloud to his family on Sunday evenings.

From the first, she loved children, and this beautiful hymn which is now before us, arose from a desire to help them in spiritual matters. It was not long before she found some of her god-children were in difficulties regarding parts of the Catechism, especially some of the Articles in the Apostles' Creed, which is contained in the heart of it. She thought that she might enlighten them if she wrote simple hymns to explain the meaning of the words. Thus a series of hymns, suitable for children, came to be written, and were included in a special collection for children.

When she came to the words, " Suffered under Pontius Pilate, was crucified, dead and buried," she had her hymn ready. She wrote " There is a green hill far away," at the bedside of a little girl who was very ill. She wanted to know about the death of our Lord Jesus Christ, so Mrs. Alexander wrote this hymn and left it with her. When she got home, she wrote it out as she had done a few hours before, in that bedroom. Thus the hymn to illustrate the words in the Creed already quoted, was lying ready to hand and was included in the collection. In the same way, in passing, we ought to note that many of her children's hymns such as " All Things Bright and Beautiful," " Once in Royal David's City," etc., were written to illustrate the Articles of the Creed.

Eventually all these hymns for young people were collected into one book, the title of which was " Hymns for Little Children "; all the profits which accrued from the publication of this hymnary, were devoted to the support of deaf mutes.

Before we look at each of the verses separately, it ought to be pointed out that this hymn had a geographical as well as a spiritual origin. Outside the city of Derry there was a striking hill which always reminded Mrs. Alexander of the place called Calvary. It lay a little beyond the city wall and it always brought to her mind " the place of the skull," " without a city wall," the city wall of Jerusalem.

VERSE 1: There are many hills we can pass by, hills which

we need never look at a second time — not so this one.
Nobody can afford to pass by this hill; it is there the dear Lord
was crucified. All of us need to go to that spot again and
again. Wicked men compelled Christ to carry His cross outside
the city, in this way most marvellously He fulfilled the Old
Testament type, suffering without the gate.

Also it is helpful to see that Christianity is founded on fact.
It is no mere theory. It is broad-based upon what happened.
That spot is dear to God, it is dear to His followers. Is it
precious to you? Whether we believe or not, there He died
and in that death the wages of sin were fully and finally paid
— He died to save us all.

VERSE 2: We can never fathom the depths of the pains He
had to bear. Besides physical and mental suffering, there was
spiritual agony. There is no more painful death than crucifixion;
that is in the physical realm. The desertion of His disciples
must have caused Him mental pain. But then too there is the
spiritual side: " My God, My God, why hast Thou forsaken
Me?" His Father's face was hidden from Him; He was the
Lamb bearing away the sin of the world; and it was for us.
What a precious assurance that is. It was for us, so we cannot
go on in our lives just as if it were not; we must seek to live
out our lives as His slaves.

VERSE 3: Before there can be any goodness, there must be
forgiveness. This order is most significant:

> " He died that we might be forgiven,
> He died to make us good."

There is no forgiveness apart from Christ's death; this was
part of its mighty purpose. How could God pass sin by without dealing with it and punishing? Being the Holy One He is,
He could never condone it. God was in Christ reconciling the
world unto Himself. Forgiveness leads to Goodness, and Goodness will end in Happiness in Heaven — " saved by His precious
Blood."

VERSE 4: If the price of sin were to be paid, it must be
paid by One who had no sin of His own to be dealt with. But
there was no one good enough to do this. But Christ was, and
being without sin, therefore He can buy us with the price of His
own life-blood. By His full, perfect and sufficient Sacrifice He

has unlocked the gate of Heaven to all believers. Have you entered through the open door?

VERSE 5: The hymn ends upon the note of appeal, and the appeal is unique and compelling. Who can resist it? His love is a "dearly, dearly" love, as a little girl once said. Greater love hath no man than this that a man lay down his life for his friends. And love ought never to be one-sided — there must be response. R.S.V.P. We *must* love Him, because He has loved us, and because if we do not we are lost and altogether undone. Let us trust in His redeeming Blood; let us be like those people in Egypt, who trusted in the Passover-blood of the slain lamb and were delivered. Once we have trusted we can try — the order is vitally important and essential. And as we try, we will remember His promise when He said, " And greater works than these shall ye do, because I go to the Father."

For all the saints, who from their labours rest

WILLIAM WALSHAM HOW
1823-1897

For all the saints, who from their labours rest,
Who Thee by faith before the world confess'd,
Thy name, O Jesus, be for ever bless'd.
Alleluia!

Thou wast their rock, their fortress, and their might:
Thou, Lord, their Captain in the well-fought fight;
Thou, in the darkness drear, their one true light.
Alleluia!

O may Thy soldiers, faithful, true and bold,
Fight as the saints who nobly fought of old,
And win, with them, the victors' crown of gold.
Alleluia!

O blest Communion, fellowship divine!
We feebly struggle, they in glory shine;
Yet all are one in Thee, for all are Thine.
Alleluia!

And when the strife is fierce, the warfare long,
Steals on the ear the distant triumph-song,
And hearts are brave again, and arms are strong.
Alleluia!

The golden evening brightens in the west:
Soon, soon to faithful warriors cometh rest;
Sweet is the calm of Paradise the bless'd.

Alleluia!

But lo, there breaks a yet more glorious day:
The saints triumphant rise in bright array;
The King of Glory passes on His way.

Alleluia!

From earth's wide bounds, from ocean's farthest coast,
Through gates of pearl streams in the countless host,
Singing to Father, Son, and Holy Ghost.

Alleluia!

OTHER HYMNS BY W. W. HOW:

O Jesus Thou Art Standing.
We Give Thee but Thine Own.
O Word of God Incarnate.
Who is This, so Weak and Helpless?

TUNES: *For All the Saints* (Barnby).
Sine Nomine.

THERE are some hymns which are made by the tunes to which they are always sung. This is one of such. For many years it was sung to Joseph Barnby's pensive tune, " Pro Omni-ubs Sanctis," but this was replaced in the first world war by Dr. Vaughan Williams' stirring composition, " Sine Nomine." But quite apart from the tune, this is an outstanding hymn; it is perhaps the best in the Church triumphant. One can never sing it without hearts being brave again and arms strengthened. Probably John Julian was referring to this hymn when he wrote in his dictionary, " Without any claims to rank as a poet, in the sense in which Cowper and Montgomery were poets, he has sung us songs which will probably outlive all his other living works."

He was born and educated at Shrewsbury, and took his degree in 1845 from Wadham College, Oxford. Ordained soon afterwards to a curacy in Shrewsbury, he was soon preferred to the Rectory of Whittington in Shropshire and then to St. Andrews Under Wall, London. So outstanding was his work that he was chosen as a Suffragan Bishop in East London, and then Diocesan Bishop of Wakefield. " Walsham How, of saintly memory, was a man of great personal piety, which shewed transparently in him. It characterized all his widely read writings; his well-known hymns are fraught with it. All brought into contact with him were conscious of it."

He was very fond of children, for whom he wrote some beautiful hymns. Those who are familiar with the hymn beginning, " It is a thing most wonderful," can never forget it :

" It is a thing most wonderful
          Almost too wonderful to be,
     That God's own Son should come from heaven,
          And die to save a child like me.

And yet I know that it is true;
          He came to this poor world below,
     And wept, and toil'd and mourn'd, and died,
          Only because He loved me so.

I cannot tell how He could love
          A child so weak and full of sin;
     His love must be most wonderful,
          If He could die my love to win.

I sometimes think about the cross,
          And shut my eyes, and try to see,
     The cruel nails, and crown of thorns,
          And Jesus crucified for me :

But, even could I see Him die,
          I could but see a little part
     Of that great love, which, like a fire,
          Is always burning in His heart.

It is most wonderful to know
          His love for me so free and sure;
     But 'tis more wonderful to see
          My love for Him so faint and poor.

And yet I want to love Thee, Lord;
          Oh, light the flame within my heart,
     And I will love Thee more and more,
          Until I see Thee as Thou art.

He also had a great gift for writing beautiful and penetrating prayers. Take this one, " A Prayer for the Parish " :

" O Lord, look down in mercy upon this Parish, and forgive us our grievous sins. Root out from among us especially the deadly sins of drunkenness and unchastity. May many souls be turned to Thee. Bless those who love Thee, and do Thou keep all those who are walking in the way of life steadfast unto the end. Give patience to the sick and afflicted, and make their sufferings a blessing to them. Bless to us all the means of grace. Prosper Thy servants in His holy work. And in Thine own good time heal all our divisions, and make us one; through Jesus Christ our Lord. Amen."

His commentary on the four Gospels for the S.P.C.K. set of volumes on the Bible is most helpful, but it is hard to come by. It combines clear exposition with spiritual depth.

Dean Pigou, the Vicar of Halifax, refers to his sense of humour. He was very fond of fishing expeditions in Ireland, whence he brought back many good stories. Stopping at an hotel where he had been before, he asked for a particular porter. One standing by and hearing him said: " Your Reverence, Was it that ye forgot to tip him? For if you did, I'm the man you're seeking for."

Let us group together some of the verses in this grand hymn. Verses 1-3 bid us consider the battle which the saints of old have fought, a consideration which is to nerve us for the fray. Verse 4 stands alone and gives us a vision of the saints in glory. The last four verses describe that yet more glorious day, the anticipation of which stimulates and strengthens the Church militant when it is inclined to flag.

The final verse in this section is, in my judgment, the most magnificent climax found in any hymn yet written. Can anyone think of a better finale? It has a transporting effect, we are carried through the gates of pearl with that triumphant host which no man can number, who shall sing God's praise for ever and ever.

There is little doubt that Dr. Boyd Carpenter had this hymn in mind when referring to Walsham How after his Home-call. He said: " He who has given a hymn to the world that can be sung by multitudes or read in the quiet of one's own chamber, confers an enviable gift upon the Church."

Let me pick out something that compels attention from each of the three groups:

(1) " Thou wast their rock, their fortress and their might." These words are taken from the opening section of Psalm 18. The Lord is my rock, my fortress, my strength. Thus we see that the inspiration of this hymn is derived from the inspired

Word of God. " I will love Thee, O Lord, my strength." Here is the secret not only of life but victory too.

(2) " One in Thee, in blest communion, fellowship divine." " They are gone but I've not lost them," said a sorely burdened man to me one day, having lost wife and daughter in one terrible week. The communion of saints in which we believe! Christ holds our blessed dead with one of His hands and us with the other. They shine, we struggle, but there's shining even in the struggle.

(3) " The King of Glory." No longer the name inscribed above the Cross in that hour of shame, but the King of Glory. Psalm 24 comes to mind. He passes on His way to the final victory, the distant triumphant song of which comes stealing on our ears even now, nerving the arm, and bracing the heart as it does so. There's only one word on which to end! ALLELUIA!

At even, ere the sun was set

HENRY TWELLS
1823-1900

At even, ere the sun was set,
    The sick, O Lord, around Thee lay;
O, in what divers pains they met!
    O, with what joy they went away!

Once more 'tis eventide, and we,
    Oppress'd with various ills, draw near:
What if Thy form we cannot see?
    We know and feel that Thou art here.

O Saviour Christ, our woes dispel;
    For some are sick, and some are sad,
And some have never loved Thee well,
    And some have lost the love they had;

And some are pressed with worldly care;
    And some are tried with sinful doubt;
And some such grievous passions tear
    That only Thou canst cast them out.

And some have found the world is vain,
    Yet from the world they break not free;
And some have friends who give them pain,
    Yet have not sought a friend in Thee.

And none, O Lord, have perfect rest,
    For none are wholly free from sin;
And they, who fain would serve Thee best,
    Are conscious most of wrong within.

O Saviour Christ, Thou too art Man;
    Thou hast been troubled, tempted, tried;
Thy kind but searching glance can scan
    The very wounds that shame would hide.

Thy touch has still its ancient power;
    No word from Thee can fruitless fall;
Hear in this solemn evening hour,
    And in Thy mercy heal us all.

OTHER HYMNS BY HENRY TWELLS:
The Voice of God's Creation Found Me.
Glorious is Thy Name, O Lord.
TUNE: *Angelus.*

THE circumstances in which a hymn was written are always matters of interest. Some hymns (like Toplady's " Rock of Ages ") were written in a makeshift shelter during a storm, a cleft in a rock; some (like Alford's " Forward Be Our Watchword ") were written while walking; some (like Henry Lyte's " Abide with Me ") while sitting quietly overlooking the sea. And so we might go on. But who ever heard of a hymn being written while invigilating an examination in a room full of boys! This surely is unique. But this is the origin of Canon Henry Twells' lovely evening hymn.

In a letter he makes this quite plain. Perhaps I had better quote it. It will put the matter beyond dispute. The author writes:

" It was written in 1868, at the request of Sir Henry Baker, who said a new evening hymn was wanted for the first edition of Hymns Ancient and Modern, and being at that time headmaster of a large grammar school — the Godolphin School, Hammersmith — I wrote it one afternoon while the boys were under examination (paper work), and I was supposed to be seeing ' all fair '. I am afraid I could not have been very energetic or lynx-eyed in my duties that day, but I little anticipated the popularity the hymn would attain. I have been asked for leave to insert it in 147 different hymnals in all parts of the English-speaking world, and many more have taken it without leave. Copies have been kindly sent to me in Greek, Latin, German, French, Welsh, and Irish. I like to think it may have brought souls nearer Christ, and if so, I heartily thank God for it."

After reading these lines we can never say again that it is impossible to do two things at once! But the character of these circumstances makes the character of the hymn all the more remarkable. It may be, of course, that the vision of a class full of boys brought home to Canon Twells the " various ills " that flesh is heir to.

Born in 1823, Henry Twells was educated at King Edward School, Birmingham, the headmaster of which was Dr. Prince Lee, one of the most outstanding men of the century. On his gravestone stands one Greek word, chosen at his own request, " Salpisei " — the trumpet shall sound. I always feel that this gives us much insight into the man's character. From Birmingham Twells went to Cambridge, and was afterwards ordained to the ministry. He held several posts before becoming headmaster of Godolphin School, Hammersmith (1856-1870). The hymn was written in 1868 while he was there. It was while he was Vicar of Waltham-on-the-Wolds, near Melton Mowbray, that Bishop Magee made him a Canon of Peterborough. He spent the last ten years of his life at Bournemouth, where he built the Church of St. Augustine at his own expense and acted as Vicar-designate until his death in 1900.

Another hymn of his with a most suitable tune, begins, " The Voice God's Creation found me." This deserves to be better known than it is. It has been included in some recent hymn books and can be introduced as an anthem.

The anonymous lines sometimes seen on sundials are usually attributed to Canon Twells:

> " When as a child I laughed and wept,
>   Time crept;
> When as a youth, I dreamed and talked,
>   Time walked;
> When I became a full grown man;
>   Time ran;
> As old still I daily pen,
>   Time flew;
> Soon shall I find in travelling on,
>   Time gone,
> O Christ, wilt Thou have saved me then?
>   Amen.

E

Froude, the historian, said of Newman as a preacher: " He seemed to be addressing the most secret consciousness of each one of us, as the eyes of a portrait appear to look at every person in the room." This hymn is as comprehensive and all-surveying as that. Let us look at it verse by verse.

(1) The whole hymn, and this verse especially, is based on the line in the Gospels in Mark 1: 32. " And at even when the sun did set, they brought unto Him all that were diseased." We see the crowds coming and then going. But then, how differently! With their divers troubles they came to Jesus, they left united and filled with joy and gratitude.

(2) This verse stamps the hymn as one specially for the evening, the time when Christ so often worked His miracles. Maybe, when the day's work is over and we are tired, we feel the need of Him all the more, and He is near, although we cannot see Him, because He has promised His presence where two or three meet in His name.

(3) Verse 3 is a prayer, indeed every verse is, after the first two, which are introductory. It is a prayer to the Saviour Christ, who said, " Ask and ye shall receive." The last two lines are very searching: " Have I ever loved Him in response to His great love, or have I lost the love I had?"

(4) We do not always find these words in the hymn; the verse is sometimes omitted to shorten it, but the words are very beautiful and true. I like the words in the last line, " only Thou." The uniqueness of Christ. " There is none other name under Heaven given among men whereby we must be saved." See Psalm 4: 8, " Thou, Lord, only."

(5) A world that cannot satisfy unforsaken. A friend that can satisfy unsought. Thus this verse may be summed up.

(6) How true this is. The nearer we are to the presence of our Redeemer, the more we feel our sin. The opposite is true. If we do not feel our sin at all, we must be far from Him.

(7) Yes, He is still man — the Son of Man (Rev. 1) — and so, approachable. We cannot find anyone who understands us half so well. Was ever mother kinder, tenderer than He?

(8) A grand conclusion, often quoted, never found to fail. His touch, His word, His mercy. He longs to make His ancient power a modern power in all our lives.

Eternal Father, strong to save

WILLIAM WHITING
1825-1878

Eternal Father, strong to save,
   Whose arm doth bind the restless wave,
Who bidst the mighty ocean deep
   Its own appointed limits keep;
      O hear us when we cry to Thee
      For those in peril on the sea.

O Saviour, whose almighty word
   The winds and waves submissive heard,
Who walkedst on the foaming deep,
   And calm amid its rage didst sleep;
      O hear us when we cry to Thee
      For those in peril on the sea.

O sacred Spirit, who didst brood
   Upon the chaos dark and rude,
Who bid its angry tumult cease,
   And give for wild confusion peace;
      O hear us when we cry to Thee
      For those in peril on the sea.

O Trinity of love and power,
   Our brethren shield in danger's hour;
From rock and tempest, fire and foe,
   Protect them wheresoe'er they go;
      And ever let there rise to Thee
      Glad hymns of praise from land and sea.

OTHER HYMNS BY W. WHITING:

O Lord, the Heavens Thy Power Display.
When Jesus Christ Was Crucified.

TUNE: *Melita.*

"WE had a Church Parade on Sunday in our Atlantic Bay. The President came on board the Quarter Deck of the 'Prince of Wales', where there mingled together many hundreds of American and British sailors and marines . . . We sang 'Onward, Christian Soldiers' and 'Eternal Father, Strong to Save,' and indeed, I felt that this was no vain presumption, but that we had a right to feel we were serving a cause for the sake of which a trumpet has sounded on high." 24th Aug., 1941.

These are the words of the Rt. Hon. Sir Winston Churchill after that momentous meeting. We can imagine sailors and soldiers and airmen joining in these and other such hymns in those tremendous days. What a good thing the hymns were ready for use, the one now to be considered having been written about seventy years before that united service.

One personal memory that I have of the hymn was singing it Sunday by Sunday, after the evening service was over, on our knees within the sound of the waves in North Devon. It made a profound impression and seemed to express the longing of every heart. It was the late Bishop of Exeter, Dr. E. H. Bickersteth, who pointed out that it was not specially suited for singing *by* those at sea, being much more appropriate when sung *for* those at sea. Thus he wrote a hymn for use at sea:

> " Almighty Father, hear our cry,
>   As o'er the trackless deep we roam:
>   Be Thou our haven always nigh,
>   On homeless waters, Thou our home.

William Whiting's great hymn will certainly be sung as long as men go down to the sea in ships. The tune " Melita " is a rousing one and specially suited to it, being composed by Dr. Dykes and named after the island where St. Paul was shipwrecked.

William Whiting was born in London on 1st November, 1825, and went to school at Clapham. For some time, later on, he was headmaster of the Winchester College Choristers' School. Besides writing many hymns, most of which have fallen into oblivion, he wrote many poems, two of which should be mentioned: " Edgar Thorpe, or The Warfare of Life " and " Rural Thoughts and Scenes." But William Whiting will be remembered for this one composition, and in this way he will share the experience of many another; for instance, John Bunyan (*Pilgrim's Progress*) and Robert Pollock (*The Course of Time*).

It appears that the hymn arose out of difficulties experienced during a storm at sea, though details as to place and time have vanished as far as I can tell. But it must be obvious that the sea is in this hymn as in few others. It is surprising that so few hymns of the sea have been written by such an " island " people as ourselves. This may account for the popularity of this hymn, though I would not decry the sheer merit of these four verses for a moment.

Sir Evelyn Wood expresses the conviction of most of us when he says: " The hymn is with me a very great favourite: it is much used by those at sea, and, when the wind blows hard, by those on land."

Besides being a Trinitarian hymn, it has many links with Scripture; Psalm 107 and several passages in the Gospels come to mind. At the end of Mark 4 we see how a great storm became a great calm at the command of the Lord Jesus Christ.

Sailors, of course, often make this hymn their first choice for hymns in any circumstances. As for instance, when I was asked for it by a young sailor who was getting married and came to see me to fix up the details. Waving aside the hymn suggested by his bride-to-be, he said, " I think we should have ' Eternal Father, Strong to Save.' " Then he glimpsed his mistake which was confirmed when I said, " But you are now going to sail into the calm haven of matrimony and are no longer in peril on the sea." A good laugh followed and he added, " Yes, I think we had better keep that for another occasion."

(1) *Prayer to God the Father.* It is because " The Lord on high is mightier than the mighty waves of the sea " (Psa. 93: 4), that we can appeal to Him in our helplessness. What a comfort this is, for the sea is full of terrors. It can never be mastered. The conquest of mountain and air and sea have gone a long way, but that over the latter is least sure. The verse on which this prayer is based is Jer. 5: 22: " Will ye not tremble at My presence, which have placed the sand for the bound of the sea by a perpetual decree." He keeps back the sea by sand — the mighty defeated by the minute, at God's word. Surely prayer will be heard.

(2) *Prayer to God the Son.* Study Mark 5: 35-41 in connection with this verse. Quite exhausted He had fallen into a deep sleep from which they woke Him thoroughly, and He said: " Silence! Be muzzled!" And the wind grew tired, and a great calm happened, and no swell for hours, as usual.

(3) *Prayer to God the Holy Spirit.* This verse takes us back to Gen. 1: 2, where the Spirit of God brooded (as a mother bird) over the face of the waters. Such a God can hear and answer our cry, and we can plead with Him, " You did it before."

(4) *Prayer to the Trinity.* The extent of the need — Rock, Tempest, Fire, Foe, is matched, and more than matched, by the love and power of our Triune God.

> Thus evermore shall rise to Thee,
> Glad hymns of praise from land and sea.

The day Thou gavest, Lord, is ended

JOHN ELLERTON
1826-1893

The day Thou gavest, Lord, is ended,
　　The darkness falls at Thy behest;
To Thee our morning hymns ascended
　　Thy praise shall hallow now our rest.

We thank Thee that Thy Church unsleeping,
　　While earth rolls onward into light,
Through all the world her watch is keeping,
　　And rests not now by day or night.

As o'er each continent and island
　　The dawn leads on another day,
The voice of prayer is never silent,
　　Nor dies the strain of praise away.

The sun, that bids us rest, is waking
　　Our brethren 'neath the western sky,
And hour by hour fresh lips are making
　　Thy wondrous doings heard on high.

So be it, Lord; Thy throne shall never,
　　Like earth's proud empires, pass away;
But stand, and rule, and grow for ever,
　　Till all Thy creatures own Thy sway.

OTHER HYMNS BY JOHN ELLERTON:

Saviour Again to Thy Dear Name.
Throned Upon the Awful Tree.

TUNES:　*St. Clement.*
　　　　Radford.

THE " Shadows of Life!" We all know something of these, and John Ellerton may be regarded as the hymn writer of the " Shadows." He had great sympathy with all sufferers and all in darkness. And his children's hymns, which are excellent in quality, are an attempt, and a most successful one, to lead children out of the shadows of fear and doubt into the sunshine of God's love. " He loves the fading light and the peace of even." Thus his hymns are summarized, and the tribute is not very wide of the mark. I have selected this hymn because it is one of our most beautiful evening hymns, which carries the " peace of even " into the soul, and enables us to leave the house of prayer with the peace of God which passes all understanding filling our hearts.

This hymn is certainly among the best three evening hymns, and one feels that this is due to the fact that events in sacred history and in daily life are handled in such a way as make one feel that God's presence is always near. His words are always simple, his rhymes natural, and his instructions easily grasped. " Saviour again to Thy dear name we raise " and " Welcome happy morning, age to age shall sing," together with the hymn we are looking at, are hymns which never fail. Are they not among the best for Congregational use? Do they not always give pleasure when sung at an open-air or in a broadcast service? One feels that John Ellerton was gifted with a sympathetic understanding of the whole of mankind, especially in its more pensive moods. Matthew Arnold considered him " the greatest of living hymn writers."

Let me tell you something of his life and labours. He was born in London in 1826 and educated at Trinity College, Cambridge. Ordained in 1850 to the Anglican ministry, he was successively curate at Eastbourne and Brighton. In 1860 we find him Vicar of Crewe Green and Chaplain to Lord Crewe. His last incumbency was at White Roding in 1886. He published a very important children's hymn book in 1859 called " Hymns for Schools and Bible Classes." He worked as co-editor with Bishop How of S.P.C.K. Church Hymns, 1871. In the course of his long life he made some very interesting notes on some of the older hymns. He wrote about 50 hymns himself and translated 10 others. He died at his post, having worked on faithfully to the end.

It is said that when lying half unconscious on his deathbed, hymns flowed from his lips in a never-ending stream. They were ever his joy and he loved to hear others sing. He was markedly reticent about his own hymns. It is interesting that like J. M. Neale he disliked the idea of copyright in connection with hymns. " If counted worthy to contribute to Christ's praise in the congregation, we ought to feel very thankful and very humble."

I must mention one of his children's hymns which was written to be sung daily at the opening of the National School in Brighton. The first verse is:

> Day by day we magnify Thee
>   When our hymn in school we raise.
> Daily work begun and ended,
>   With the daily voice of praise.

He was widely known and loved, being a man of deep culture, tender feeling and great personal charm. One says of him, " He was always making the best of and doing the best for others, never thinking of himself."

Note:—

(1) *God's Sovereignty*: This is how the hymn begins: it begins with God — The day Thou gavest . . . Thy behest . . . Thy praise. When one knows God is Sovereign and Father all is well, everything works together for good. Morning light and evening darkness are both under His control as well as everything else.

(2) *God's Church*: This is made up of all faithful people throughout the world, of every clime and every colour. It is very moving to remember that the Church in this sense is un-sleeping: they are always there awake to watch and pray. The world Church is a fact at which we rejoice.

(3) *God's ear*: He listens and there are always some every-where to praise and to pray. We praise Him for all that is past and thank Him for all that is to come. How often as we sing this verse we say to ourselves, " Praise and prayer must make up my life henceforth."

(4) *God's Works*: But it is not *our* doings, but His which form the theme of our praise and prayer. All that we do is nothing worth except God blesses the deed. In this verse we have a perfect example of the simplicity of Ellerton's hymns. There is not a word or a line a child cannot understand.

(5) *God's Throne*: All through the hymn there has been the thought that time is passing, day and night come and go with amazing rapidity. Time is so temporary! But there's one thing

that does not pass away, one empire is present, and that is God's Kingdom established around His everlasting throne. "Heaven and earth shall pass away," Christ said, "but My word shall never pass away." Included in Christ's word there is God's Throne and God's Kingdom.

"Thy throne, O God, is for and ever" (Psa. 45: 6).

"Thy Kingdom is an everlasting kingdom, and Thy dominion endureth throughout all generations" (Psa. 145: 13).

Now the day is over

SABINE BARING GOULD
1834-1924

Now the day is over,
    Night is drawing nigh,
Shadows of the evening
    Steal across the sky.

Now the darkness gathers,
    Stars their watches keep,
Birds, and beasts, and flowers
    Soon will be asleep.

Jesus, give the weary
    Calm and sweet repose;
With Thy tenderest blessing
    May mine eyelids close.

Grant to little children
    Visions bright of Thee;
Guard the sailors tossing
    On the deep blue sea.

Comfort every sufferer
    Watching late in pain;
Those who plan some evil
    From their sin restrain.

Through the long night watches
    May Thine angels spread
Their white wings above me,
    Watching round my bed.

When the morning wakens,
    Then may I arise
Pure, and fresh, and sinless
    In Thy holy eyes.

Glory to the Father,
    Glory to the Son,
And to Thee, blest Spirit,
    Whilst all ages run.

OTHER HYMNS BY S. BARING GOULD:

On the Resurrection Morning.
Through the Night of Doubt and Sorrow.
Onward, Christian Soldiers.

TUNES :   *Eudoxia.*
           Lyndhurst.

IT does not often happen that a hymn is written to fit a tune. As a rule it is just the other way round. In some cases the hymn or poem lies fallow, as it were, for some time before a suitable tune brings it into prominence. But in the case of this hymn, and also " Onward, Christian Soldiers," and the children's hymn, " Daily, Daily, Sing the Praises," the tune came first. Baring Gould had the tunes and he wanted to use them at his Mission at Horbury Bridge in 1865. Thus the lines were written. One would scarcely credit it because there is such spontaneity in all three hymns. But thus it was.

Sabine Baring Gould was born at Exeter on 28th January, 1834, educated at Cambridge, ordained in 1864 to the curacy of Horbury near Wakefield. In 1867 he became Vicar of Dalton, Yorks.; from there he was preferred to West Mersea in Essex in 1871; thence to the Rectory of Lew Trenchard in Devon, which he held until his retirement.

Throughout his life he was a voluminous writer. His chief works are " The Lives of the Saints " (15 volumes); " Curious Myths of the Middle Ages," 1866; " The Origin and Development of Religious Belief," 1869. And there were also several volumes of sermons and other smaller works. He found great recreation in his literary work, and has left the Church a great legacy.

Besides the hymn before us there are several others very well known. " Onward, Christian Soldiers " was written during the night of the children's procession round the park on Whit-Sunday, 1865. " Through the Night of Doubt and Sorrow " was a translation he made from Ingemann's fine Danish hymn. " On the Resurrection Morning " was written as an Easter hymn to illustrate the clause in the Creed, " I believe in the Resurrection of the Dead."

He was a man of great industry, as can be imagined from the works I have mentioned as coming from his pen. When asked for his secret, he replied: " The secret is simply that I stick to a task when I begin it! And, it would never do to wait from day to day for some moments which might seem favourable for work."

The story of his courtship and marriage is very touching. While a Curate at Horbury he fell in love with Grace Taylor, the daughter of a mill hand. Her parents agreed to the sug-gestion that she should be sent away for a time to be educated. When she returned from college they were married, and it proved to be a very happy union. When she died in 1916, eight years before his own Home-call, he had inscribed on her tombstone, " Half my soul."

The hymn which we are noticing is one of the best evening hymns for children which we have. It was written in 1865 at about the same time as " Onward, Christian Soldiers." The simplicity and picturesqueness of the hymn make a deep appeal to children. It has become known in all English-speaking countries and has been translated into several foreign languages. It was founded on the text, Proverbs 3: 24, " When thou liest down, thou shalt not be afraid; yea, thou shalt lie down, and thy sleep shall be sweet."

The hymn printed at the head of this study is full of God's tenderest blessing. It begins at nightfall and after mentioning sundry dangers and hardships, it brings us to the light of morn-ing. Children, sailors, sufferers, evil-doers, angels — none are forgotten, and the hymn ends with a Doxology to the Holy Trinity.

In the course of the hymn there are several words and phrases which appeal to children. Here are some: " stars begin to peep," " mine eyelids," " visions bright," " the deep blue sea," " the angels' white wings," " fresh." One feels that the realism of the hymn is part of its attraction, together with glowing appreciation of nature in its many-sidedness. The hymn has the singular power of carrying those who use it to the various scenes mentioned — the sailors in their ships, the sufferers in their pain, the wicked in their plots. What a lovely ascription at the end for us to use as we fall asleep, perhaps having used the hymn in our prayers:

> Glory to the Father,
>   Glory to the Son,
> And to Thee, blest Spirit,
>   Whilst all ages run.

Tell me the old, old story

KATHERINE HANKEY
1834-1911

Tell me the old, old story,
    Of unseen things above,
Of Jesus and His glory,
    Of Jesus and His love.
Tell me the story simply,
    As to a little child,
For I am weak and weary,
    And helpless and defiled.

Tell me the story slowly,
    That I may take it in:
That wonderful redemption,
    God's remedy for sin.
Tell me the story often,
    For I forget so soon;
The early dew of morning
    Has passed away at noon.

Tell me the story softly,
    With earnest tones and grave;
Remember, I'm the sinner
    Whom Jesus came to save.
Tell me that story always,
    If you would really be,
In any time of trouble,
    A comforter to me.

Tell me the same old story,
    When you have cause to fear
That this world's empty glory
    Is costing me too dear.
Yes, and when that world's glory
    Is dawning on my soul,
Tell me the old, old story:
    " Christ Jesus makes thee whole."

ANOTHER HYMN BY KATHERINE HANKEY:
I Love to Tell the Story.
TUNE: *Gospel.*

IN our own minds some hymns are associated with particular experiences. In the early days of my ministry I remember going to Banbury to speak at some special meetings, and I was entertained to lunch and tea by three charming Quaker sisters, all of whom were elderly. It was a Quaker home on the old style and I recall that we stood for grace before the meal and we held hands around the table, while the eldest sister said to the youngest, " Rachel, wilt thou please give thanks." Much of their conversation was in Bible language, and I call to mind that I first heard the word " vexed " used there in the sense the Psalmist used it.

Well, before I left that home they gave me a copy of a little booklet in the circulation of which they were very interested. They told me it had already appeared in many languages and was soon to appear in others. It was entitled " The Old, Old Story." That little book I have still and it is a prized possession, and I thank God upon every remembrance of Miss Braithwaite who gave it to me.

It is made up of 56 verses and is in two parts, " The Story Wanted " and " The Story Told." The date of the first is 29th January, 1866, the second, 18th November, 1866. It is from this larger piece that our hymn is taken, and a refrain has been added, as I shall explain later.

It may be that you will wish to know how the hymn originated and how it began to circulate in this and other lands. During the 1859 Revival in Ireland, an old minister was visited by a younger one who brought news of the Revival. When the news of the awakening had been given, the invalid, who was dying, said: " Tell me the old, old story, and nothing else."

Miss Braithwaite tells how in 1866, the year of publication, a friend, Benjamin Seebohm, gave to her brother George, who was then five, a copy of " The Old, Old Story," saying: " Here is a little book for a little boy; I will put his name upon it and I hope that as soon as he is old enough he will learn it by heart."

That little ½d. book was treasured and learnt by heart. When George Braithwaite grew older he became a commercial traveller. He often spent his pocket money in buying more copies of the little book which he gave away on railway journeys.

Not much is known of Miss Hankey, but I have come across a letter from her niece, Miss Agnes E. Rashdall, which contains such valuable information that I must give it in full:

" I think probably few people in these days would know that the hymn was originally written as the introduction to a tiny booklet in verse, published in, or about, 1868, under the title ' The Old, Old Story,' the eight verses of the hymn having the heading ' The Story Wanted,' and the remainder ' The Story Told." (Some ten months elapsed between the writing of the first and second parts).

It gives in very simple form the story of Redemption, starting with the Garden of Eden, going on to the Nativity and the announcement to the shepherds of the fulfilment of the promise; the kind of life lived by our Lord, His character, His death and His resurrection; and, finally, the personal message to ourselves.

The little book seemed just to meet the need of the time, and for a great many years had a very remarkable circulation. (It is even now not actually out of print, but is still issued by Longman's as a penny booklet). It was also translated into several European languages, and into others used in mission fields of Asia and Africa. Miss Hankey herself wrote music for it, but the tune usually used now for the hymn is not hers.

Miss Hankey wrote a number of other hymns, mostly not intended or suited for congregational use, though one or two are to be found in some hymn books, and she also published a book called ' Bible Class Teachings,' now out of print.

She was always warmly interested in religious teaching, and when quite young herself, gathered together a Bible Class of business young women, going round to the shops, under her mother's escort, to give personal invitations. It was much appreciated, and some of its members became life-long friends and themselves undertook Christian work. It was probably her varied experiences in teaching which specially helped her to put the deepest religious truths into the very simple language of ' The Old, Old Story.'

Kate Hankey's life was an uneventful one, and there is little to record. Her father, Thomas Hankey, was a banker, and in her early years she lived at Coombe House, near Croydon, but later on her home was always in London. She was one of a large family, and had a religious upbringing, Mr. Hankey being a member of the Evangelical group which people used to call the ' Clapham Sect.' And at her boarding-school she came under the influence of Mr. Vaughan of Brighton, whose teaching of young people was a marked feature of his ministry.

After the move to London she always associated herself with the work of the parish in which she was living, and for several years worked under the Rev. G. H. Wilkinson — afterwards Bishop of Truro — who became a much valued pastor and friend.

Owing to home ties, her life was a very quiet one, and the specially marked incident in it was a voyage to South Africa to bring home an invalid brother. The long journey alone up-country was at that time somewhat of an adventure for one with very little experience of travel, and the kind help of clergy and missionaries to whom she had introductions, and all that she learnt of their work, led to her taking for the rest of her life a keen interest in foreign mission work.

She died in 1911, at the age of seventy-seven."

Dr. W. H. Doane, the American composer, wrote the tune to which it is usually sung and added the refrain. It came about in an extraordinary way. A certain Major-Gen. Russell, whose name was familiar in connection with the quelling of riots in Ireland, attended a great Y.M.C.A. Convention at Montreal in Canada. Before a large audience he read out this poem, which made a profound impression. Dr. Doane was present and was very drawn to the poem. He obtained a copy and when travelling later by stage coach in the White Mountains the music came to him.

The appeal of the hymn, as Julian says, lies in " its great beauty and simplicity," and also one feels, in its personal appeal. Christ and the individual soul are brought together. " Tell ME . . . of Jesus. Tell ME . . . Christ Jesus makes THEE whole."

Take my Life

FRANCES RIDLEY HAVERGAL
1836-1879

Take my life, and let it be
Consecrated, Lord, to Thee;
Take my moments and my days,
Let them flow in ceaseless praise.

Take my hands, and let them move
At the impulse of Thy love;
Take my feet, and let them be
Swift and beautiful for Thee.

Take my voice, and let me sing
Always, only, for my King;
Take my lips, and let them be
Fill'd with messages from Thee.

Take my silver and my gold,
Not a mite would I withhold;
Take my intellect, and use
Every power as Thou shalt choose.

Take my will, and make it Thine;
It shall be no longer mine;
Take my heart, it is Thine own;
It shall be Thy royal throne.

Take my love; my Lord, I pour
At Thy feet its treasured store:
Take myself, and I will be,
Ever, only, all, for Thee.

OTHER HYMNS BY F. R. HAVERGAL:

Lord, Speak to Me that I May Speak.
I Could Not Do Without Thee.

TUNES: *Mozart.*
             Consecration.

THERE is a story behind this moving hymn as with most hymns. When in her early thirties Miss Havergal went to stay with some friends at Areley House for a few days; there were ten persons in the house, some Christians who were unhappy, and others unconverted, whose lives had been made the subject of prayer.

Let me give you her own words: " God gave me the prayer: ' Lord, give me all in this house.' And He just did; before I left the house every one had got a blessing. The last night of my visit, after I had retired, the governess asked me to go to the two daughters. They were crying; then and there both of them trusted the Lord and began to rejoice. It was nearly mid-night. I was too happy to sleep and passed most of the night in praise and renewal of my own consecration, and these little couplets formed themselves and chimed in my heart one after another, till they finished with ' Ever, only, all for Thee."

It is very striking to notice how in each of the twelve couplets of this poem, the combination of "my Lord" and "myself" recurs. It ought to be carefully noted because it is full of devotional helpfulness. " My life . . . consecrated to *Thee;*" " My hands . . . *Thy* love;" " My voice . . . *my King;*" " My will . . . *Thine;*" " My love . . . *Thy feet;*" " Myself . . . *Thee.*" These are just a few of the pairs which might be picked out. Christ has a claim upon every part of us; all to Him I owe.

This is one of the most fluent hymns one could ever read through. It is a thing of beauty which will be a joy for ever. I believe this hymn has proved to be one that is easily transla-table. The smooth flow of this hymn has rarely been equalled and never excelled. It is a masterpiece. It is not surprising that one authority speaks of it as " one of the most beautiful and best-loved hymns " in existence.

After the writing of this hymn, she sang only for Jesus Christ. This was in December, 1873. In August, 1878, she wrote to a friend: " The Lord has shown me another little step, and of course I have taken it with extreme delight. ' Take my silver and my gold ' now means shipping off all my ornaments to the C.M.S. (including a jewel cabinet that is really fit for a countess)."

Miss Havergal wrote a precious book, entitled " Kept for the Master's Use "; it is a commentary on this hymn and is one of the most helpful books that can be found on the subject of consecration and full surrender.

The hymn itself is a prayer, an appeal, an offering. It is the response of one who feels that nothing can be held back because Christ gave all.

He gave His life — " The Good Shepherd giveth His life for the sheep." It was given not for friends, but for enemies, and given without reserve.   There we see the greatest gift Deity could offer; and such a giving of His life demands my soul, my life, my all!   There is no alternative.   Thou art worthy to receive, — take my life.

Take my hands: Think of His hands, they were pierced with nails; but it was love and not the nails that held Him on the Cross.   Those tender, faithful, strong, open hands they smashed with huge iron stakes which they drove ruthlessly through the quivering flesh.   And as they did so, He prayed, " Father forgive them, for they know not what they do."   Can we do anything else than place our hands in His in loving, glad allegiance?

Yes, and our voices must be His too, for we have heard His voice.   The words which He spake were not His, but the Father's which sent Him.   " As we sing," Frances Ridley Havergal used to say, " let us look up to Him for His smile.   In this way our songs reach more hearts than finer words unaccompanied by His power."

Take my heart, my love, myself . . . Nothing less will do because He gave us His heart.   " Behold . . . He is mighty . . in heart," says Job (36: 5, margin).   And this mighty, tender heart loves us with an everlasting love.   He died of a broken heart for you —

> " Take my heart; it is Thine own;
> It shall by Thy royal throne."

Let me close by telling you how it all began with Frances Ridley Havergal, how she first yieded her heart to Christ.   She was the daughter of a clergyman, and from her earliest years she had a deep interest in the things of God, especially the meaning of the Lord's Supper.   A sermon by a curate in Worcester on the text, " Fear not, little flock," impressed her deeply, and she spoke to him, but he was an unskilled adviser and could not help her to find Christ.

In February, 1851, with a very heavy heart, she came to Okehampton, " longing to know she was forgiven."   Before long a Miss Cooke became her confidante, and one day, after a long conversation, she asked, " Why cannot you trust yourself to your Saviour at once?"   " I can."   Hurrying upstairs she committed her soul to the Saviour, and she came down later feeling she did trust in Christ.   This is the source of the stream, since then the blessing has flowed on and on.

Miss Havergal had copies made of her Consecration Hymn which she often used in her meetings. She used to ask those to whom God had spoken to sign their names at the bottom as a pledge of their resolves to be " Ever, only, all for Jesus."

Will you write out the hymn and sign it?

As with gladness men of old

WILLIAM CHATTERTON DIX
1837-1898

As with gladness men of old
Did the guiding star behold;
As with joy they hail'd its light,
Leading onward, beaming bright;
So, most gracious Lord, may we
Evermore be led to Thee.

As with joyful steps they sped
To that lowly manger-bed,
There to bend the knee before
Him whom heaven and earth adore;
So may we with willing feet
Ever seek the mercy-seat.

As they offer'd gifts most rare
At that manger rude and bare;
So may we with holy joy,
Pure and free from sin's alloy,
All our costliest treasures bring,
Christ, to Thee, our heavenly King.

Holy Jesus, every day
Keep us in the narrow way;
And, when earthly things are past,
Bring our ransom'd souls at last
Where they need no star to guide,
Where no clouds Thy glory hide.

In the heavenly country bright
Need they no created light;
Thou its light, its joy, its crown,
Thou its sun which goes not down;
There for ever may we sing
Hallelujahs to our King.

OTHER HYMNS BY W. C. DIX:

Come Unto Me, Ye Weary.
To Thee, O Lord, Our Hearts We Raise.
Joy Fills Our Inmost Hearts Today

TUNE: *Dix.*

THERE are at least three remarkable things about this hymn. First, it was written during recovery from a serious illness. This is an unusual origin for a hymn and is worth noting. How few of us would think of writing a hymn at such a time; we prefer to hear them being sung. Secondly it arose out of a time of meditation upon a passage of Holy Scripture. It was the Feast of Epiphany, 6th January, and feeling a little better, Dix was reading Matthew 2: 1-12. He felt that there were many lessons to be learnt from the adoration of the wise men which had not been put into verse, so he immediately began to muse on the subject and the result was this hymn. You will notice the thought of edification all through . . . As . . . So may we. As . . . So may we. Then, thirdly, it was the work of a layman. Has it ever struck you how many of our best known and loved hymns were written by ministers of the gospel? The Church owes a great debt to her clergy in this respect. The hymn before us is the work of a layman, however, and it is interesting to say the least, on this account.

The hymn was brought into prominence and its place established as one of our outstanding hymns by reference being made to it by Lord Welbourne at the Church Congress in 1866. He was speaking on the subject of English Church Hymnary and said: " Of writers still living, I do not feel called upon to make myself, in this place, either a critic or a eulogist. But I may be permitted to say that the most favourable hopes may be entertained for the future prospects of British Hymnary, when among its most recent fruits is a work so admirable in every respect as the Epiphany Hymn of Mr. Chatterton Dix, ' As with Gladness . . . ' "

W. C. Dix was born in Bristol in 1837, the son of a surgeon, John Dix, who was very fond of the poems of Thomas Chatterton. He named his son " Chatterton " after his favourite poet, and, indeed, wrote a *Life of Thomas Chatterton*, which has been one of our chief sources of information about that rather pathetic poet. Dix was educated at Bristol Grammar School and looked forward to the life of a sailor in the Merchant Navy. But delicate health made this impossible, and we find him for many years associated with the marine insurance office. Facts about his life are few and far between, but he has left behind him the reputation of a godly churchman who was widely respected for the consistency of his Christian life.

His hymns appeared first in smaller collections and in his two devotional works, " Light " and " The Risen Life," and a book of instruction for children entitled " The Pattern of Life." The last named contains some very beautiful hymns for children. The hymn we are considering is a great favourite with children, especially to the tune " Dix." It was circulated, to begin with, in a small collection of hymns for private use only, entitled " Hymns of Love and Joy," and then found its way into Hymns Ancient and Modern in 1861.

Mention of the tune reminds me of its interesting origin. It was written in 1838 by Conrad Kocher, a German composer, in the form of a chorale. Dix himself did not like the tune, may- be because it is not sufficiently meditative, but admitted some years afterwards that, " now nothing will displace it."

Dix also followed another rather unusual line. He was very fond of versifying translations of services connected with other Churches for instance, services in Greek and Abyssinian Churches. In 1863 Dr. Littledale brought out translations from the Greek which he called " Offices of the Eastern Churches." Many of these Dix turned into metrical form and they are excellent.

Julian rightly esteems Dix's hymns very highly. He says they are " of value . . . many rank high among modern hymns." He instances the one before us and the plaintive " Come Unto Me, Ye Weary," which reminds us of Bonar's " I Heard the Voice of Jesus Say " and Neale's " Art Thou Weary, Art Thou Languid." There are about thirty of Dix's hymns in common use, of which six or seven are outstanding.

As we look through the hymn we can see there is a slightly different thought in each verse, and they mount up more and more until we come to what Dix himself calls " heavenly country " — a lovely conception. The story of the Magi is simply told and the application is made as we go along. It is clearly and beautifully done. Is there any hymn where there is a more effective combination of truth and teaching?

VERSE 1. *The thought of guidance.* It is possible that the ancestors of the Magi received the information about the star from their forefathers, who got it originally from Balaam — " There shall come a star out of Jacob." It is probable that the prophecy was again brought to their notice by Israelites of the Captivity and the Dispersion. In any case they saw an unusual star and, feeling it was a divine signal, they followed it and it led them to Christ. They obeyed with joy, and their quest brought them to Him. In just the same way God gives us a measure of light, and if we follow the gleam it will bring us to Christ. There are many ways to Christ, but only one to God (John 14: 6).

VERSE 2. *The thought of adoration.* Again the thought of joy is present. What a happy thing it is to be a Christian. But the main emphasis is upon adoration and worship. When we find Him we must bend the knee and everything else must bow. What a privilege it is to adore Him with the whole company of heaven! But don't come now to any lowly bed but to the mercy seat. The former was only temporary and a stepping stone to the latter. Let us come boldly, that is, telling Him everything.

VERSE 3. *The thought of giving.* It would appear that the wise men did not actually visit the stable and find Christ in the manger. The Holy Family had moved to the " house " which is specially mentioned. But this is a minor point. The main thought is that they offered their gifts. It is interesting to recall that on the Feast of Epiphany at the Chapel Royal, the reigning monarch has always presented 25 golden sovereigns, together with two little bags of frankincense and myrrh, to be given as part of the offering. It is afterwards distributed among the poor. So may we bring our best to offer to Him.

VERSE 4. *The thought of preservation.* Here we see the pathway of faith ending in sight as St. Paul saw it would (1 Cor. 13: 12). And in this pathway we pray to be kept as the wise men were. They arrived, and by God's grace so will we. " We shall see Him as He is." Saved from wrath through the mediation of a Saviour who died (the ransom), we are being saved and shall be saved by His life, for He ever liveth to take care of us and our needs.

VERSE 5. *The thought of heaven.* When the sun rises then the stars disappear. This is the thought of the last verse. They need no light there, for the Lamb is the light thereof. How gloriously the thought is expressed that Heaven is Jesus Christ, and Jesus Christ is Heaven. " To depart, and be with Christ, which is very far better."

> " The road to Heaven lies through Heaven,
> And all the way to Heaven is Heaven."

The Church's one foundation

SAMUEL JOHN STONE
1839-1900

The Church's one foundation
    Is Jesus Christ her Lord;
She is His new creation
    By water and the word:
From heaven He came and sought her
    To be His holy bride
With His own blood He bought her,
    And for her life He died.

Elect from every nation,
    Yet one o'er all the earth,
Her charter of salvation
    One Lord, one faith, one birth;
One holy Name she blesses,
    Partakes one holy food,
And to one hope she presses
    With every grace endued.

Though with a scornful wonder
    Men see her sore opprest,
By schisms rent asunder,
    By heresies distrest:
Yet saints their watch are keeping,
    Their cry goes up, " How long?"
And soon the night of weeping
    Shall be the morn of song.

'Mid toil and tribulation,
    And tumults of her war,
She waits the consummation
    Of peace for evermore;
Till with the vision glorious
    Her longing eyes are blest,
And the great church victorious
    Shall be the church at rest.

Yet she on earth hath union
    With God the Three in One,
And mystic sweet communion
    With those whose rest is won:
O happy ones and holy!
    Lord, give us grace that we,
Like them, the meek and lowly,
    On high may dwell with Thee.

OTHER HYMNS BY S. J. STONE:
Weary of Earth and Laden with My Sin.
Lord Christ My Master Dear.

TUNE: *Aurelia.*

Many of Frances Alexander's best hymns were written to elucidate the Catechism, in such a way that children who learnt it would understand it the better. It was Sir Wm. Robertson Nicoll who said that we must teach our children their Catechism by means of hymns. Now besides Mrs. Alexander, Mr. Stone decided to do this, and the hymn before us is part of the result of this plan.

It was written to illustrate the ninth article of the Creed — " The Holy Catholic Church — the Communion of Saints." " Weary of earth and laden with my sin " was the text in order and connected with " The Forgiveness of Sins." They were all produced at the time of Bishop Colenso's evolutionary views on the Bible; they were to constitute a kind of defence of the Church doctrine. Mr. Stone himself has given some account of their production, and it may be wise to include this here.

" They were written at Windsor when I was Curate there in 1866, and finished off immediately after, during a holiday at Margate, and a few months after published with ten others (the twelve making one each on the twelve articles of the Apostles' Creed) in a little volume called " Lyra Fidelium." I wrote them all in behalf of the poorer people in my country district, who I found in many cases used the Creed in their prayers with but little comprehension of it. When I wrote " The Church's One Foundation," the steadfast defence of the Faith made by Bishop Gray of Cape Town against the heresies of Colenso some time before was much in my mind. I am personally most thankful about " Weary of Earth," because of the private testimonies I have had of its use in bringing home to individual souls the doctrine of the atonement. One such was to this effect, a poor dying woman told a lady who visited her daily that her favourite verse, ' the lines that comfort me and make me ready and happy to go,' was the fourth, beginning, ' It is the voice of Jesus that I hear." '

It has probably exerted a more powerful influence and stirred more enthusiasm than any piece of prose written in defence of the Church. It is often sung at Church congresses and conferences and never fails to unite men together in faith and endeavour. One writer says it " puts a new song in our mouth which makes us incapable of accepting defeat." It is a hymn for grand occasions. It is reckoned to be one of which the leaders of the Church are very fond.

Archbishop Temple once said that whenever he preached in a country Church he could always count on two things — cold chicken and "The Church's One Foundation"!

Samuel John Stone was born in Staffordshire in 1839, and after a distinguished career at Oxford he was ordained on a title to the curacy of Windsor Parish Church; in 1870 he became curate of St. Paul's, Haggerston, where he succeeded his father in 1874. For the last ten years of his life he was Rector of All Hallows, London Wall.

We can see something of the opportunities of modern evangelism in one of his remarkable efforts. He discovered that many factory girls were coming up to London very early on cheap trains, and had nothing to do and nowhere to go. He decided to open his Church and hall so that a service could be held, and then the young women could go to the adjoining building to read and sew and wait till they had to leave for work. "We shall never get the outsiders in, until we who are in go out," said John Wesley. Stone saw this and made his plans accordingly.

Some 48 hymns are listed by Dr. Julian as in common use of which he says, "The greater part are strongly outspoken utterances of a man's faith, where dogma, prayer and praise are interwoven with much skill. Usually the keynote is 'hope.'" One of his hymns, "Lord of Our Soul's Salvation," was ordered by command of Queen Victoria to be sung at the thanksgiving for the recovery of H.R.H. the Prince of Wales, on February 27th, 1872.

"Always improving" might be written over all Stone's hymns, for none of them is now sung as originally written. He was always making emendations and improvements. Besides altering words, he often added verses. The hymn we are now going to consider is in three forms. In 1866 it appeared in seven stanzas; the revised form in 1868 in five stanzas; and an expanded form in 1885 in ten stanzas to be used in great processions in Salisbury Cathedral.

Instead of looking at the verses in detail let us concentrate upon the doctrine they contain of which Stone was so fond. The "Church" is the dominant truth here.

We see:—

(1) *Its origin.* Her foundation is Jesus Christ her Lord. In Acts 4: 12 we read, "There is none other name under Heaven

given among men whereby we must be saved.   1 Corinthians 3:
11: " Other foundation can no man lay than that is laid, Jesus
Christ " our Lord. To change the figure — Christ came to seek
His bride for which He was content to pay such a great price.
With his own blood He bought her and for her life He died!
In the fourth line of verse 1 there is reference to Baptism and
the Ministry of the Word. Of all the verses this is the most
perfect and most comprehensive and often brings tears to one's
eyes.

(2) *Its unity.* As His new creation there is necessarily a
unity which is divine. One, one, one, one . . . the word occurs
again and again. And the oneness of our life is not forgotten,
the blessed Hope to which she presses. The unity of the Church
is the unity of the family, elect from every nation; which has not
to be created but kept. " Keep the unity of the Spirit." And
the Church is not divided although part have crossed the flood.
There is the Church triumphant as well as the Church militant.

(3) *Its difficulties.* Because of the enemy of souls there are
difficulties, many and various. There is heresy, schism, oppres-
sion, tears and the like. But all these things drive us back into
the Foundation where every foe is vanquished and Christ is
Lord indeed. Christ is the answer and He is prominent in every
single verse of the hymn.

Over the hymn Stone quotes the verse, Acts 20: 28: " The
Church of God, which He hath purchased with His own blood."

O Love that wilt not let me go

GEORGE MATHESON
1842-1906

O Love, that wilt not let me go,
    I rest my weary soul in Thee;
I give Thee back the life I owe
That in Thine ocean depths its flow
    May richer, fuller be.

O Light, that followest all my way
    I yield my flick'ring torch to Thee
My heart restores its borrow'd ray,
That in Thy sunshine's blaze its day
    May brighter, fairer be.

O Joy, that seekest me through pain,
 I cannot close my heart to Thee;
I trace the rainbow through the rain,
And feel the promise is not vain
 That morn shall tearless be.

O Cross, that liftest up my head,
 I dare not ask to fly from Thee;
I lay in dust life's glory dead,
And from the ground there blossoms red
 Life that shall endless be.

OTHER HYMNS BY GEORGE MATHESON:
Make Me a Captive, Lord.
Gather Us In.

TUNES: *St. Margaret.*
Hampstead.

SOME of our greatest hymns were written in the furnace of
 trial and bodily suffering. This is true of George Matheson,
whose best-known hymn, " O Love that wilt not let me go," was
written after he had lost his sight at 20 years of age. His
blindness links him with John Milton, Fanny Crosby and other
distinguished blind writers.

You will probably note the undertone of anguish in the words
of this hymn, but you will also catch the song of hope and
trust. As we read, we feel something of the storm, but we also
see the rainbow. Tragedy is transformed into triumph by the
power of Christ. Matheson speaks of tears, pain, weariness and
a flickering torch, but also of love, light, joy, the Cross.

There is undoubtedly *one* tragedy connected with this hymn,
possibly *two*.

While still young, during his brilliant student days, Matheson
lost his sight. What a handicap! But it did not overwhelm
him. The hymn was written, he tells us, " in the Manse of my
former parish, Innellan, one summer evening in 1882. It was
composed with extreme rapidity . . . I was suffering from extreme
mental distress, and the hymn was the fruit of pain."

These words suggest a second tragedy. It must be clearly
stated that this is not so well authenticated as the blindness, and
all the distress connected with it, but it must be mentioned. It
is said that when his fiancée knew of his blindness, she broke
off the engagement, to his great sorrow. " I cannot marry a

blind man," she said, and so she gave him up. This hymn may have been written with this episode in mind. The " mental distress " would be the keen remembrance of what took place twenty years before. The opening of the first verse, " O love that wilt not let me go," fits well into this framework. The character and tone of the hymn, harmonises with the nature of this disaster.

The more one thinks of the Rev. George Matheson, the eager student robbed of his sight, the active minister robbed of his mobility, the sensitive lover robbed of his lady — the more one is conscious of the nobility and grandeur of the man. Yet he would be the first to renounce any praise or glory; like the preacher who was thanked for his address at Keswick, he would have said, " I'll pass it on to Him."

With these things in mind let us turn to the hymn itself to examine each verse in detail.

(1) " O love that wilt not let me go " — Such is the heart of the loving Shepherd — He will never forsake us. He seeks and searches till He finds the wandering sheep. All others may forsake, He never will. In such a love there is rest. There cannot be rest except in Him who said, " Come unto Me and I will give you rest." But love's demands are deep, its claims sweeping. We owe our life to this Lover of souls, and it must be given back to Him. If we launch out into the ocean of God's love, fulness and wealth are inevitable. The majestic tide is a symbol of power. Into that channel our life is to flow.

(2) " O Light that followest all my way." As we grope in the darkness we are not left alone; a light follows us. It is the light of the world. The light of the world is Jesus. Our own light is a poor thing, a mere flickering torch; Christ is the source of all light. We catch the note of humility in the words, " My heart restores its borrowed ray." What is borrowed is not our own; life is a loan; we ought to be thankful for it. As we place our flickering torch — the heart itself — into His keeping, we come into the sunshine; the Sun of Righteousness scatters all the shadows, and light divine and perfect is our portion.

(3) The third verse begins as the other three do with an exclamation: " O Joy that seekest me through pain." Here we discover the deepest meaning of pain. Pain is a pathway along which someone comes seeking me. I cannot close my heart to Thee — Love incarnate, Love divine, Joy ineffable. What the

rainbow is to the rain, that the promises of God are in our experience. For more than 20 years Matheson had not seen a rainbow, but he relied on the promise. Morn shall tearless be. " In the morning," we read at the end of St. John's Gospel, " Jesus stood on the shore." " God shall wipe away all tears from their eyes."

This is the appropriate place in this short meditation to point out that Dr. A. L. Peace wrote a special tune for this hymn. It is called " St. Margaret," and it is in the fullest harmony with the sentiments expressed. The music fits the message of each verse, but none more perfectly than verse 3.

(4) The amazing compassion of the Saviour can have but one effect: it humbles us; we bow our heads; pride is brought low; we lay in dust life's glory, dead; we count all things but loss that we may win Christ. And in that hour the Cross comes before us and Life is bestowed — life that shall endless be.

Let me close with a beautiful prayer by George Matheson, culled from his book, " Moments in the Mount": " O God, Thou living God, let me fall into Thy hands; it is only in Thy hand that I can be perfectly safe. There is a pain with Thee which is not found without Thee, but it is the pain of love which is the pain of life Divine; translate me into that life. Lift me into union with Thy divine Being. Take me into Thy hands and hold me in Thy fear; let me learn in Thy life how solemn is my own, let me see in Thy glory how poor is my own, through Jesus Christ our Lord. Amen."

INDEX OF HYMNS MENTIONED

INDEX OF HYMNS MENTIONED (Continued)